KNITTED GARDENS

Front and back cover: Everywhere the eye wanders over this
beautiful bedspread, some small, delightful detail captures
the imagination. It can be made to any size and worked as a
group project. (Also see pages 20 and 21.)

KNITTED GARDENS

Imaginative designs, practical and decorative, all with a garden flavour.

Jan Messent

SEARCH PRESS

Published in Great Britain as *Jan Messent's Knitted Gardens* 2007
Search Press Limited,
Wellwood, North Farm Road
Tunbridge Wells, Kent TN2 3DR

Reprinted 2007, 2008, 2009

Originally Published in 1991 as *Knitted Gardens*

Reprinted 1997

Photographs by Search Press Studios

Photograph of 'Crocus Field' by Anne Coleman

The author would like to acknowledge that in preparing this book she
has been extremely fortunate to have had the help of good friends,
who took on some of the more time-consuming projects. To Brenda
Pearson, whose knitting needles clicked away from dawn to dusk
over a period of months, she gives special thanks. To Anne Coleman,
Sandra Goode and Victoria MacLeod, warmest thanks are also given
for their generous contributions. The help of the following five yarn
spinners is acknowledged in producing these projects: - Dunlicraft
(DMC threads), Emu Wools, Hayfield Ltd., Patons and Twilleys
(Goldfingering metallic threads). Also, thanks to George, whose
garden features many times in this book.

Finally, thanks must be expressed to past students at the Knitting
Craft Group workshops, who contributed ideas and know-how on
the subject of knitted gardens. It is to these students that this book
is lovingly dedicated in the hope that it will bring back memories of
hilarious days when they wallowed knee-deep in yarns to produce
gardens of delight.

ISBN: 978 1 84448 183 5

Printed in Malaysia

CONTENTS

Introduction

Introduction

It is inevitable that a teacher will absorb many ideas from her students, in the same way that they absorb hers. Suggestions passed on in the most casual way, like seeds tossed into the wind, often grow and bear fruit after a remarkably quick germination in the fertile mind, proving time and time again that, with the right conditions, stimulus, materials and time, a surge of creativity can be unleashed positive enough to amaze even the creator. I have seen it happen so many times; the glow of achievement when, after just two or three days, a stunning project has materialised from someone who, until then, had had no reason to believe in her own creative ability. Yes, maybe a hesitant admission to being able to knit, just, but never to having made anything. How that creative experience has generated a new confidence and given a glimpse of a child-like joy at the results of sheer nonsensical indulgence! And then to discover that others like the results too! They warm, unbend and giggle and, for a few moments, become child-like too, and then relax into play-time with all the seriousness of an imaginative toddler, like men playing with train-sets and sailing model boats. The creative knitter has the ability, like Alice, to shrink into her knitted greenhouse and arrange her knitted plants in her knitted plant-pots, and give not one more thought to who it is *really* for! Well, of course, we can always say, (if pressed), that it is for a child we know, but secretly we suspect that the recipient will never derive as much pleasure from it as the one who imagined, planned and made it.

The material in this book is the result of many years spent in teaching school-teachers how to pass on the skills of knitting to children. This was where ideas were tossed about, caught, mulled-over and brought to fruition. But, whereas my students were able to work on their ideas while they were still 'hot', I had to wait, sometimes years, before digging mine out of cold-storage and nurturing them back to growth. Fortunately, I made many scribbled notes after classes and so was able to retrieve ideas and instructions aeons old.

One of the themes most recently tackled was 'knitted gardens' and so packed with possibilities was this that I was convinced the ideas should go into a book. Many people will recognise details as being similar to ones they produced during workshops. This will come as no surprise to them, as they willingly gave me permission to make free with any suitable material and develop it, re-shape or blatantly copy it, such is the generosity of the teaching profession. Some ideas withered on the stony ground of my memory and some died due to my lack of skill so, in cases like this, I have brought them back in the form of illustrations without instructions, so that knitters more skilled than I am may be able to try them out.

This is no ordinary knitting book, that much will be obvious, but not only for its subject-matter. A certain chattiness has crept into the instructions, just as though author and reader were attending an informal workshop where several alternative solutions to each problem can usually be found. To creative people, lateral thinking is the norm, as there is rarely only one way of doing something. Hence my alternatives dotted about at random amongst the greenery pages, my 'try it out and see if it works' approach, which I believe is far more conducive to real creativity than pages of inflexible instructions. In short, I prefer my reader to make some decisions of her own! All the instructions given here are elastic ones, made to be adapted and given a new and unique life of their own under your hands. Stretch and bend them, turn them face about and 'do your own thing' – this is the way to produce a garden which is truly yours.

This subject lends itself to ideas which are far too numerous to put into so few pages, for gardens change with the seasons. Imagine your summer garden but under snow and ice, with a snowman on the lawn and icicles hanging from the eaves. Imagine the November bonfire and fallen leaves, or the new pale-greens of spring. Imagine a water-garden with bridges, and little grottoes with statuary and Greek urns full of flowers, and white temples where crinolined ladies sweep in and out. Japanese gardens, parterre gardens, the Chelsea Flower Show, Italian gardens, the flower shop, the greengrocer's stall at the market – what colour, what shape to knit! Keep your camera handy, and a sketch-book, a scrap-book of pictures and a notebook for experiments, (you'll wish you'd written it down at the time), and keep looking. Wander in and out of my pages and watch what *these* gardeners are up to, then stealthily lay out your yarns, needles and tape-measure and set to work.

The structure of the book is a personal one, being based on the assumption that creative knitters prefer a choice in how they build, furnish and people their own ideal garden. With this in mind, my chapters follow the same concept of first building the garden to a scale and design based on personal requirements and/or skills. The units suggested in the first chapter will hopefully provide enough ideas to enable the knitter to find suitable ways of making translations which are both decorative and functional. Having decided on the 'ground plan', the next stage is to add material from the second chapter; maybe a greenhouse and cold frame, garden bench and fountain, or tools and plants. The latter will, naturally, determine the kind of garden to be grown. Trees and hedges, walls and fences are available to enclose and to partition the plots, and cottages can be built without even a suggestion of planning permission! The choices are entirely your own and will depend on your time, commitment and skills; choose how big you wish your garden to be and then stop, or develop, at any stage.

The penultimate chapter gives a variety of figures without which no garden can reach its full potential! Choose the friars of bygone days or the more contemporary people in gardening clothes: they may represent real people or imaginary characters, about whom you can weave stories for the delight of a young friend. The little pockets all round the bedspread enable you to hide things in the garden and press-studs will allow the planting and uprooting of vegetables and flowers at any stage. More details are sugested here and there, too simple even for instructions. But before you know it, those who cast a patronising eye on such unfunctional absurdities will be suggesting ways in which your garden might develop, even to the point of advising you which plants to grow and where, and reminding you of details which you should include. And *this* is the point where *you* might then acquire a spare pair of needles, just in case . . .? Ah well, maybe that's going too far! But if anyone has to hack away at the greenery to find you, blame me and mumble something about the 'Sleeping Beauty' syndrome.

Helpful hints

Before you begin on these small projects, consider how you can add your own touch of uniqueness to each one, by adapting the ideas to suit your personal requirements. The following pointers may help you to do this more easily.

How much yarn shall I need?

The quantities given here are in multiples of 25gm (1oz). However, much smaller amounts are termed 'oddments' and these may vary from a few metres (yards) to a ball the size of a golf ball. When in doubt, allow a little more than you think, as leftovers are useful for foilage and features. So, although the instructions stipulate a certain amount of yarn, exactly that amount may not be entirely used up even though this amount has to be purchased in order to complete the piece.

Use your kitchen weighing-scales to find out whether the oddments you have will add up to the required amount. As a rough guide, it takes 50gm (2oz) of double knitting yarn to make 20 × 6cm (2¼in) squares in garter stitch on size 4mm needles. Garter stitch squares made up into a panel which measures 91 × 45cm (30 × 18in) may take between 250 and 300gm (9 and 10oz) of yarn.

Variations in colour

When working on small projects, don't be too concerned about the dye-lot numbers being the same on the ball-bands. Nature is liberal with her tones of greens, browns and neutrals, and these variations make colour-schemes more interesting.

Variations in yarns

Remember that some double knitting yarns are actually thicker than others, so stitches will almost certainly have to be adjusted to obtain the correct measurements. Your own tension, or gauge, will also affect this to some extent. This is perfectly normal; simply knit a bit to find out what is happening and then, if need be, increase or decrease one or two stitches. On a largish piece you can get away with this! More than this and you may have to re-start with a different number of stitches, different yarn or needles, but *keep notes* on all changes. If you don't, you'll wish you had.

In the long run, it is always safer to make a tension square before you begin; it really does save time and effort. Check with the samples on page 120. For extra help, here are some facts against which you can check your own tension.
On size 4mm needles with double knitting yarns:–
Garter stitch will measure 5sts and 10 rows to 2.5cm (1in).
Stocking stitch will measure 5sts and 8 rows to 2.5cm (1in).
For every 7.5cm (3in) of knitting, cast on 16sts.

Variations in size

When all said and done, it won't be a disaster if your pieces turn out to be a bit smaller, or a bit larger than those in the instructions. Get into the habit of adapting the pieces you are making, and keep notes. When measuring small units, and estimating the number of rows needed, remember that the cast on and cast off rows must also be taken into account. This is why you should measure your tension from the centre of a knitted square and not along one edge.

Measurements in the book are given in both centimetres and inches: do not mix the two as they are not exact equivalents. Choose one or the other and keep to your choice throughout.

Variations in direction

In traditional knitting we have become accustomed to making items from the bottom to the top, even though we know that other directions are perfectly acceptable. The units which make up many of the projects in this book can be knitted in any direction, depending on the following:–
A. The number of stitches with which you can cope.
B. The shape of the piece.

C. The stitch pattern.

Do consider these factors before you cast on: look at the diagram of the pieces and/or the photograph and decide for yourself whether it might be easier for you to make them downwards, sideways, or to pick up stitches from an adjoining edge and just knit on. This often saves time on sewing-up!

Knitting in small units

Though it is perfectly possible and basically simple to knit, for instance, a complete garden in one large piece instead of in many separate pieces sewn together, there are advantages in making things in bits.

A. When different types and thicknesses of yarn are used in one project, the separate pieces allow you to adjust to these differences more easily, by increasing or decreasing the number of stitches and rows.

B. Small pieces are much less daunting to manage than large ones and are easier to handle and transport.

C. 'Mistakes' assume an importance relative to the scale of the work!

D. Small pieces encourage one to keep on being creative, (sometimes called changing your mind!) as you go along, making choices about colour, shape and suitability. This is much more fun than doing yards of mechanical knitting.

Sewing up

This aspect of 'unit knitting' need not deter you; for one thing if offers a respite from the physical act of knitting and, for another, it offers an exciting reward when you can see your project being built up before your eyes. I *never* recommend waiting until all the bits are done before sewing up; I can't wait that long to see how it will look! Unless it is impossible for some reason, sew the bits as you go, a few at a time. See page 126 for diagrams about which method of seaming to use.

Group work

I realise that, as a result of the ideas in this book, much of the knitting will be the work of groups, either adults or children, or both. This is another very good reason why it is easier to design large projects in units. Bear in mind, though, that if you are responsible for organising such a group of knitters, they will produce a variety of tensions. It will be helpful to them, as well as to you, to have card templates which will ensure that individuals produce the same size and shape. We all know that one person's idea of a square is not exactly the same as anothers!

Glueing

Many of the finished projects are glued to card foundations, this being a perfectly acceptable way of keeping tiny pieces of knitting rigid. There are many good craft glues available; I use pots of liquid latex-based glue, (thick white stuff), with a brush in the lid. The solid kind in sticks is not strong enough for this type of material.

Always place the glue on the card, never directly on to the knitting. Save all kinds of card pieces, rolls and tubes, foam pads and polystyrene shapes, to be used as the foundations of your inventions. Use a ruler and a *very* sharp craft knife for accuracy when cutting these foundations, and always use a cutting mat. Dotted lines on diagrams indicate lines to be scored and folded, *not* to be cut right through. This is done on the side which is to be folded *away* from you, not towards you.

Planning your garden

The function of the finished pieces is an important factor to consider. The illustrated knee rug, cushion or bedspread will give you hours of pleasure but the bedspread could just as easily be used as a chair rug; the knee rug squares made into a coat; the walled garden hanging into a bedside mat and the idea for the seed packets built into bags, garments or a set of framed pictures.

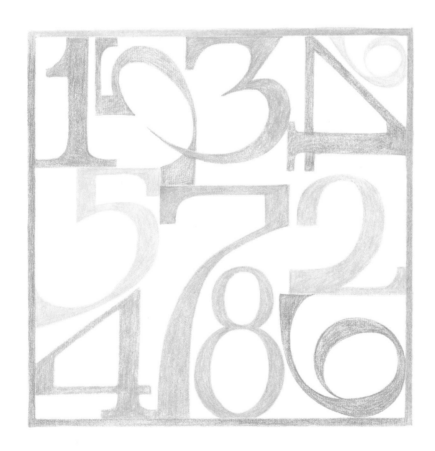

Formal garden knee rug

What at first may seem like a huge project is really only a set of squares knitted in different designs and sewn together, in fact, just a patchwork and an ideal project for taking on your travels or when visiting. The choice of how to use the squares can be left until you run out of yarn, or steam, or both! You may get as far as a bedspread, stop short at a cushion to match the knee rug, or decide on an eye-catching coat similar to the one illustrated on page 14.

As an example of how many squares you would have to make, a cushion would need eight squares, four front ones and four back ones, plus a 5cm (2in) border all round. A bedspread for a single bed would require approximately twelve pieces length-ways and nine pieces across, or a total of 108 pieces. The knee rug required forty-nine pieces, seven in each direction.

Measurements

Each square measures 18cm (7in). The completed knee rug measures 140cm (55in) square, including the border.

Materials

This knee rug for an elderly retired gardener was knitted entirely in Patons DK yarns, in seven different shades of green and grey. The precise amounts used are given below.

The amounts of yarn needed for this project will obviously depend on its size, but as a rough guide, to make three 18cm (7in) squares you will need 50gm (2oz) of assorted DK yarns in greens and greys, or any other colour combination of your choice. Whatever is left over can be used for a border to complete the edges. Any oddments of greens or neutrals can be used, providing they are of the same weight and thickness. The knitting was done on size 3¾mm needles and the border in this version was crocheted on a size 4mm crochet hook, but this can be knitted if preferred, see instructions.

Opposite: **The motifs in the knee rug were inspired by examples of shrubs and topiary, as well as formal garden arrangements. The cushion decoration was based on a vegetable plot, but you could just as easily add fruit or flowers.**

Yarns Used

Three deep greens, all Patons, but others can be substituted:–
Bottle 6956, Beehive Soft Blend DK, 3 balls.
Lovat 6949, Waverley DK Tweed, 2 balls.
Evergreen 6042, Beehive Shetland DK, 4 balls.
One mid-green:–
Sherwood 7326, Pure Wool DK, 4 balls.
Two greys:–
Flint 6945, Waverley DK Tweed, 3 balls.
Scafell 6232, Beehive DK & Mountain Wool, 3 balls.
One neutral:–
Beech 6944, Waverley DK Tweed, 4 balls.

Designs Used

Altogether 23 × 50gm (2oz) balls of DK yarns were used on 49 squares. The following explains *how* they were used, though you can vary this in any way you wish.

There are ten different designs and each of them is numbered, see Knitting charts 1 to 10. You will see that some have a motif on a background, some are made up of lines and borders and some have a definite centre and it is easy to see which is which.

With this in mind, the following list tells you which design, by number, has which colour yarn in which area, so that, if you want to follow the same colour arrangement, this will enable you to see where the colours go.

If you prefer to substitute your own colour scheme, the list above will still help you to see how much of each is required. However, it would be much more fun to make the whole thing out of oddments and play it by ear!

Colours used

Design 1: beech background, bottle motif.
Design 2: beech background, bottle motif.
Design 3: Sherwood background, bottle motif.
Design 4: Sherwood background, bottle motif.
Design 5: beech background, all 4 greens on patches.
Design 6: bottle border, Sherwood patches, beech lines.
Design 7: flint background, evergreen lines, Sherwood centre.
Design 8: Scafell background, bottle border, Sherwood lines.
Design 9: Lovat background, bottle border, Sherwood patches, Scafell lines.
Design 10: Scafell background, bottle patches, Sherwood centre.
The border takes 8 × 50gm (2oz) balls of DK yarn in any deep green.

Arrangement of squares

It is entirely for you to choose whether to knit all ten designs or just some of them. The chart, see Fig 1, shows the arrangement of the squares used in this version. They may be placed so that all the designs lie

Above: To complete a coat or jacket made from the squares, add ribbed welts and edges.

in one direction, or in both directions; as the pieces are square they should fit either way. Note that some rows are 50 rows deep and some are 51.

7	1	8	2	8	3	7
4	9	10	6	10	9	1
8	5	7	4	7	5	8
2	6	4	7	4	6	2
8	5	7	4	7	5	8
1	9	10	6	10	9	3
7	4	8	2	8	1	7

fig 1 **chart showing arrangements of designs for knee rug**

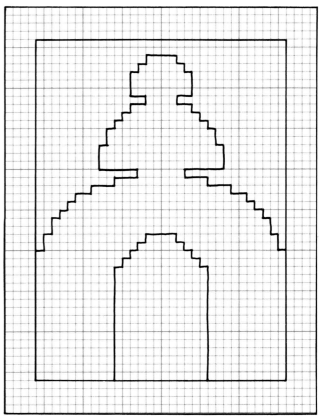

1

Border

The crochet one on the knee rug is 6.5cm (2½in) deep. First a narrow band of dark green double crochet was worked into the knitting, 175dc along each side on the first row, and making 3sts into each corner. Altogether 13 rows of dc, (i.e rounds), were made, increasing as before into each corner.

To *knit* the border, simply make narrow bands in garter, or moss st, casting on about 16sts, and sew these on as shown, see Fig 2. The corners will fit into each other without any shaping. To finish off, four corners have been embellished with pom-pons; these are for old or young fingers to play with!

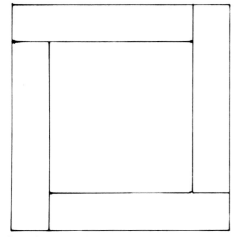

fig 2 **diagram of knitted border for knee rug**

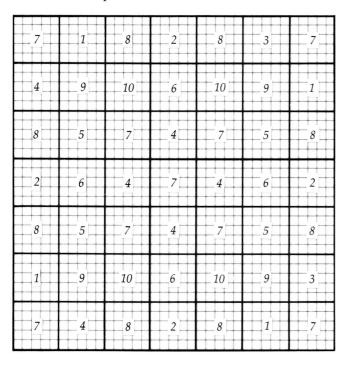

2

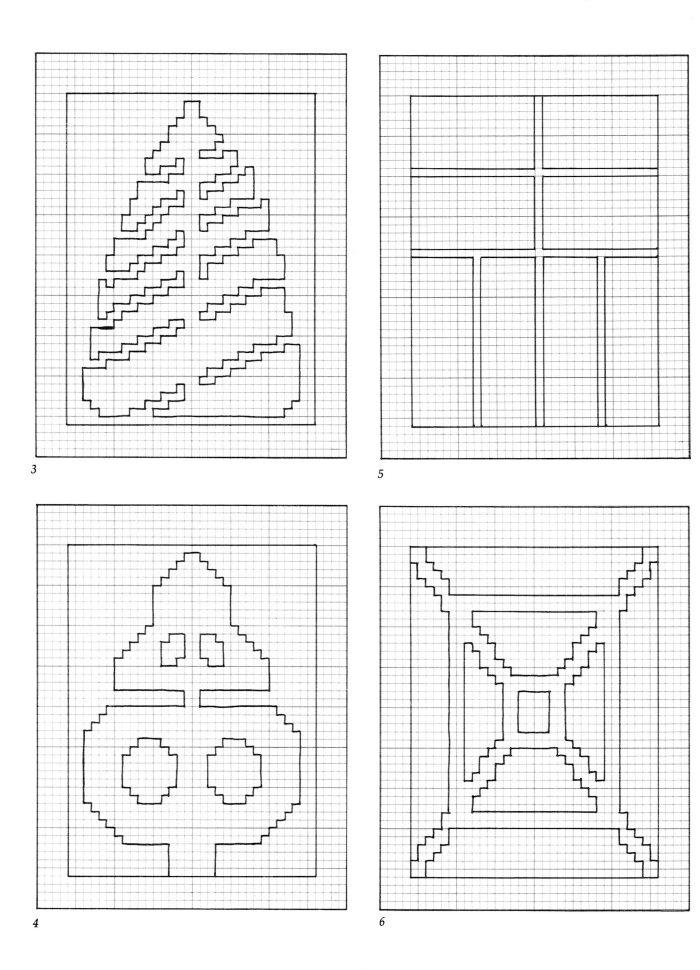

3

5

4

6

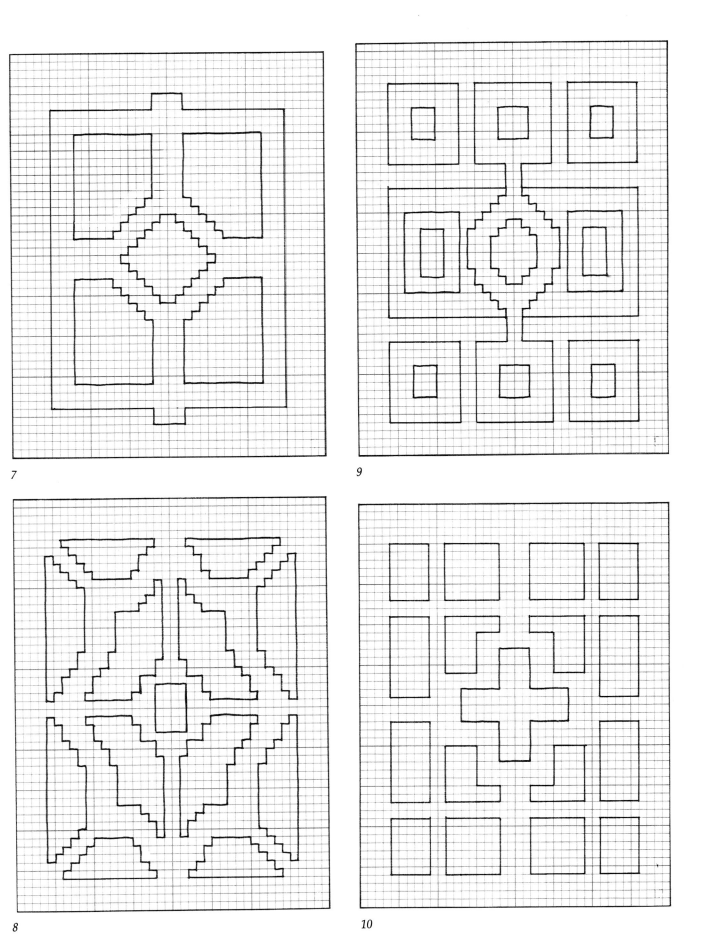

7

8

9

10

Garden cushion

This cushion is made to fit a 41cm (16in) cushion pad from a total of eight diagonal squares, four for each side, knitted in a combination of garter stitch and fur, (loop), stitch, see Fig 1. All the vegetables are made separately, and can be attached in any arrangement you choose. More squares will make a larger cushion; many squares could become a bedspread!

Materials

Use a variety of DK yarns in greens and browns totalling just over 200gm (7oz). Vegetables are made from coloured oddments.

Sizes 3¾ and 6mm needles and a 4.50mm crochet hook.

41cm (16in) cushion pad.

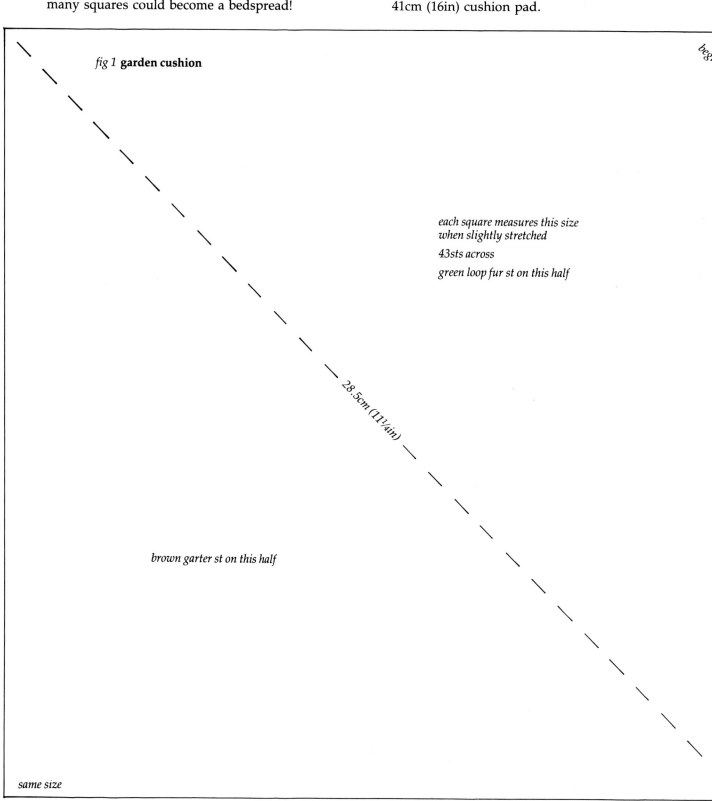

fig 1 **garden cushion**

begin

*each square measures this size
when slightly stretched*

43sts across

green loop fur st on this half

brown garter st on this half

28.5cm (11¼in)

same size

Front of the cushion

For these squares, use size 3¾mm needles and green yarn. Cast on 3 sts and knit in g st, increasing once into first and last sts of second and every alt row until there are 9 sts.

Next row: work fur, (loop), st beg with k1, see page 121.

Continue to inc as before on alt rows.

Continue in this way until there are 43 sts, changing to brown yarn on the last inc row. Knit one more row. Now change to size 6mm needles and work entirely in g st.

Next row: dec one st at each end of this and every alt row until there are 28 sts.

Change to size 3¾mm needles. Dec as before until only 12 sts rem. Knit one row. Dec at each end of *every row* until only 2 sts rem. Cast off.

Make 3 more pieces in the same way.

Instructions for the vegetables can be found on pages 85–89.

Back of the cushion

For these squares, use size 3¾mm needles and brown, green, or a mixture of the two, cast on 2 sts and knit them.

Working in g st, inc one st at each end of next and every alt row until there are 42 sts. Knit one more row. Change to a different brown or green and begin to dec one st at each end of next and every alt row to the last st. Finish off.

Make three more pieces in the same way.

Making up

For the arrangement of the squares, see Fig 2, and for a plan of the cushion complete with vegetables, see Fig 3.

After joining the squares together to make the back and the front pieces, join three of the side edges together. On the open side, RS out, work double crochet sts down both edges – about 60 sts to each side. On to the first row of crochet sts, make loops of 3ch into every 3rd chain space. Do this all the way round the opening. Make a long crochet cord of green yarn and thread this through the loops, like lacing a shoe, and tie at the corner.

fig 3 **plan of cushion complete with vegetables**

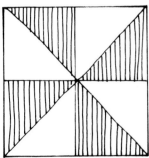
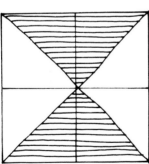

fig 2 **showing how diagonal squares can be arranged**

Garden bedspread

What better way to absorb the attentions of a small child than this garden bedspread, where little fingers can walk down the path, through the gate and on into the herb garden? The larger figures will bring the garden to life and you can give them names, take them into the house pillow or pop them into the little plant pot pockets along the borders. In this version, the plants and vegetables have been sewn on to the plots, but they can be press-studded on instead, to make them interchangeable. In this way, the plants can be gathered into a basket and replaced again overnight!

The items from chapters two and three are designed to be added to this garden, as well as to the others. A cold frame, watering can, bench and trees as well as little creatures are all essential details for the keen bedspread gardener and these will all no doubt lead to numerous stories involving the Dove family, (no relationships specified), who live in Dove Cottage (i.e the house pillow) and who also look after the friary garden.

This project grows remarkably quickly as the small units are added, especially if more than one person is involved. What's more, it is a perfect way of using up small oddments of yarn which need not all be of the same type. Bright colours will blend in with the greens and browns. If not enough greens are available, use a dye to change neutral and pale colours to a new range of green tones. This can be done and left overnight, or while you are out at work, and will produce shades which could never be purchased. Remember that only colours which are paler in tone to the colour you wish to produce will take a dye. A darker colour cannot be made into a lighter one, but random-dyed yarns are very useful.

Measurements

Overall size approximately 152 × 127cm (80 × 50in). This is large enough for a child's bed with a short drop at the sides and the end.

All measurements must be made as accurately as possible on *unstretched* fabric but note that because of the differences in yarn thickness, even within the DK range, the number of stitches and rows may have to be adjusted to make the pieces fit correctly. This is particularly so if more than one person is working on the project, as tensions differ enormously. For this reason, longer measurements have not been given in numbers of rows.

To ensure accurate results, cut pieces of card to the correct measurements and make pieces of knitting to these shapes, particularly in group work.

Materials

The completed bedspread weighs approximately 2250gm (5lb) and is clearly intended for sitting on top of, rather than lying underneath! It is only possible to give approximate amounts for the various component parts of this project, as so much depends on the type and thickness of the DK yarns used and whether one prefers to knit, crochet or mix techniques.

The following breakdown may, however, give some idea of the amounts needed, though one should always have more available just in case it is required. Don't be too particular about things like dye-lots though, or even exactly the same shade, as variations make a garden-scene much more lifelike and interesting. So, make use of all those oddments and pay keen attention to the exact *size* of the pieces, as they will have to fit together like a patchwork.

All the yarns used are DK weight unless otherwise specified. You will need:–
1000gm (2lb 3oz) assorted greens.
500gm (1lb 2oz) fawns and beiges for paths and terrace.
400gm (14oz) bright colours for pom-pons (make approximately 90).
200gm (7oz) assorted colours for fur st borders and other foliage.
100gm (4oz) rich/strong browns for plots.
50gm (2oz) for flower pot pockets on borders.
350gm (12oz) chunky-weight yarn for dark green border on size 5½mm needles.

Size 4mm needles are required unless otherwise specified, and for crochet, if any, size 4.50mm hook.

Stitches

Garter stitch is the predominant stitch used, as this produces a fabric of the correct density to withstand much handling without stretching out of shape. Moreover, the many different directions in which the small pieces are sewn helps to keep the shape admirably. Some stocking stitch is used, but only a little, and some double moss stitch for the borders. Fur, (loop), stitch for the herbaceous borders may either be knitted or crocheted, see page 121.

Crochet can be substituted for any, or all of these shapes, as they have been by me in this version. Just note the measurements and keep to them accurately. The best crochet stitches to use, either alone or in conjunction with knitting, are either double crochet or half-trebles, these being closer to the density of garter stitch than treble stitches.

Where to begin?

There is no one answer to this as, in theory, one could make all of the units in any order and then sew them all together later. But what a chore this would be for most people.

My own method was to begin in the centre, (well, to be honest, this was because I didn't have a plan to follow, and if I had I couldn't have stuck to it for long!), and in this way one can knit a bit, sew a bit, build it up and

Above: Close-up detail taken from the garden bedspread.

re-adjust things here and there, and so the project becomes more of an event, something to be referred to as 'the pre-bedspread' period or the 'ante-bedspread' period! So my advice is to begin in the centre and go on from there.

Sections shown on chart

A. The central section is a paved plot in tweedy yarn on which grows a sage bush, or other coloured foliage, see Fig 1. Knit it in ss on 20sts for 26 rows. Measurement: 9.5cm (3¾in) square.

B. Four triangles in g st with 3 tiny bushes on each one. Cast on 20sts, knit 1 row, then dec one st at each end of every alt row until 2sts rem. Cast off. Measurements: 9.5 × 7.5 × 7.5cm (3¾ × 3 × 3in).

C. Four narrow strips bordering the central square. These are pathways, so use fawn yarn and work in ss on 6 sts for about 46 rows, as follows:–
Row 1: k6.
Row 2: p1, k4, p1.
To make a ridge across, work 3 rows of p about every 8th row. The corners fit into each other as shown on the diagram.
Measurements: 2.5 × 21cm (1 × 8½in).

D. Four corner squares knitted on the diagonal in g st forming the centre corners of the brown plot. Using dark brown yarn, cast on 2sts and k.
Row 2: inc into both sts to make 4.
Row 3 and alt rows: knit.
Row 4: inc into first and last sts to make 6.
Continue in this way until there are 22sts. K one row, then dec on alt rows until 2sts rem. Cast off. Measurement: 7.5cm (3in) square.

E. A continuous row of g st squares, the centre one being a continuation of the pathway and the two side ones being part of the angled brown plot joined to (D).
In brown, cast on 15sts and k 26 rows. Change to fawn and k 26 more rows, then change back to brown and k 26 more rows. Cast off.
Measurements: 7.5 × 23cm (3 × 9in).

F. Eight diagonal squares in g st, half fawn, half brown, green or mixed colours for the flower plot. Using the same method as (D), inc from 2 to 38sts and change colours at this point. Always knit one row before beginning to dec back to 2sts. Measurement: 15cm (6in) square.

G. Four brown g st squares knitted straight to form

23

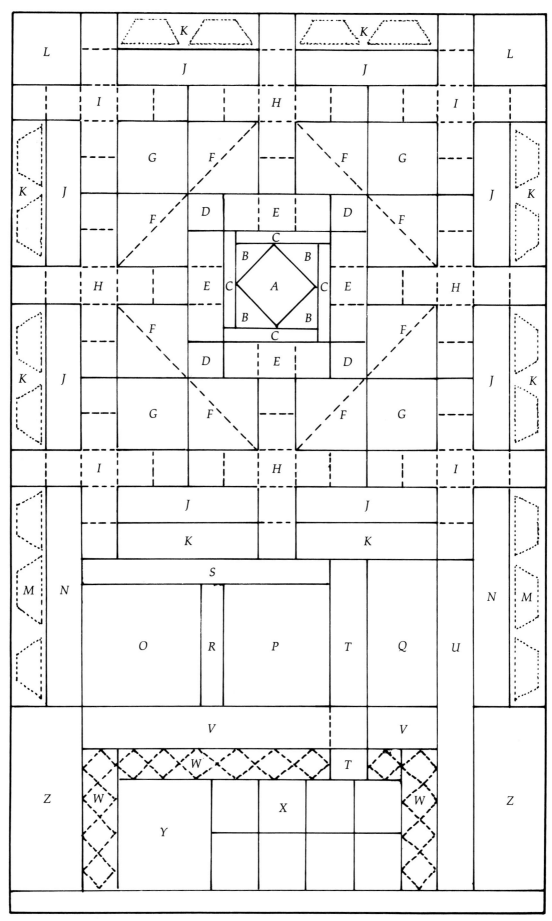

fig 1 **chart for garden bedspread**

the centre pieces of the large triangular flower plot with (F). Use the same yarn as in one half of (F) and work on 30sts for 57 rows. Cast off.
Measurement: 15cm (6in) square.

H. Four upright crosses forming pathways of chequered fawn/mossy greens, representing moss-covered stone slabs and short grass, using any oddments of green.
Make a continuous strip 15sts wide in g st of 5 squares, 26 rows each, beginning and ending with green. Then pick up 15sts along each side of the central, (green), square and knit on for 2 more squares (52 rows). If you prefer, these can be sewn on instead.
Measurements: arms of cross 15 × 7.5cm (6 × 3in).

I. These are exactly the same size and shape as (H), but only fawn paving colour is used.
For variation, the central square may be knitted on the diagonal and the four arms picked up from the edges and knitted on. For this, the diagonal central square should be increased to 20sts, then decreased back to 2sts.

J. Eight narrow herbaceous borders of brightly coloured yarns, DK, furry and textured, shiny or matt. Two or three strands are used together and thicker yarns may also be used.
With 3 strands of DK use 6mm needles. Cast on 9sts and work in fur st for 30cm (11¾in).
Measurements: 30 × 7.5cm (11¾ × 3in).

K. The eight green borders which adjoin (J) are the backgrounds on to which the plant pot pockets are sewn: They are exactly the same size as (J) and can be knitted either in g st or double moss st, as in this version.
Using DK yarn on 4mm needles, cast on 64sts and work 26 rows in double moss st. If a thicker, chunky type yarn is used instead, work on size 5mm needles and 48sts for 18 rows. For these 8 pieces, approximately 200gm (7oz) of yarn will be needed.

L. Two square corners in double moss st to match the borders.
Use DK yarn with 32sts and work 52 rows in double moss st. If chunky yarn is preferred, use size 5mm needles and 24sts and 36 rows.
Measurements: 15 × 15cm (6×6in).

M. Two longer borders to match (K), using the same yarn and same stitch. Though this is not vital, it does add to the unity of the design. These are made in the opposite direction, that is, from the narrow end.
With DK yarn, cast on 16sts and work for 46cm (18in). With thicker yarn, use 5mm needles and cast on 12sts.
Measurments: 46 × 7.5cm (18 × 3in).

N. As with (J), these longer herbaceous borders are made on size 6mm needles, 3 strands of DK, (all colours), and 9sts. Work in fur st.
Measurements: 46 × 7.5cm (18 × 3in).

O. This brown seedbed is where young plants mature ready for the lower garden.
Made in DK yarn and g st cast on 50sts and knit 106 rows, but check your own measurements to be sure. If you prefer to crochet this piece, as the one given in this version, use a 4.50mm hook, a base chain of 36sts and work in half-trebles for 30 rows, but check that the measurements are the same. For foliage, see page 90.
Measurements: 25 × 25cm (10 × 10in).

P. Another slightly smaller seedbed in brown DK.
In g st work on 45sts for 106 rows. To crochet, work in half-trebles on 32sts for 30 rows. For foliage, see page 92.
Measurements: 25 × 22.5cm (10 × 9in).

Q. A narrower seedbed in brown or dark-green DK.
In g st work on 30sts for 30cm (12in). In crochet, work on 21sts until long enough. For foliage, see page 92.
Measurements: 30 × 15cm (12 × 6in).

R. This narrow pathway joins with (S) to make a T-shape so use the same fawn DK yarn as for the other pathways. Knit in g st on 10sts for 106 rows.
Measurements: 25 × 5cm (10 × 2in).

S. The top section of the T-shaped pathway, knitted in the same yarn as (R). Work on 10st in g st for 204 rows, or as long as needed.
Measurements: 53.5 × 5cm (21 × 2in).

T. This pathway leads from the terrace, under the gate and joins (S) at one corner. All the better if you can use the same colour to link the terrace to the other pathways. Cast on 15sts and work in g st for 46cm (18in).
Measurements: 46 × 7.5cm (18 × 3in).

U. A long pathway running almost the complete length of the garden, but joining (I) midway. As before, work in g st on 15sts and make this as long as needed.
Measurements: 69 × 7.5cm (27 × 3in).

V. The trellis-work fence is made in two parts, see page 26.
Measurements: 53.5 × 9 and 15 × 9 cm (21 × 3½ and 6 × 3½in).

W. The green right-angled borders which enclose the terrace are made of narrow strips, and as they will be covered by foliage, any dark-coloured oddments of DK yarn will do. Neither does it matter in which direction you knit, sideways or lengthways.
LH side: cast on 62sts and work in g st for 29 rows. Cast off 49sts and continue on the rem 13sts for another 38cm (15in). This makes a right-angle.
RH side: cast on 62sts and work 29 rows in g st. Cast off 49sts and continue on the rem 13sts for another 30 rows or until the pathway (T) is reached. For foliage, see page 90.
Measurements: 46 × 6cm (18 × 2½in) and 29 × 7.5cm (11½ × 3in).

X. The terrace is knitted in eight oblong pieces in g st. Any stone-coloured oddments will do, preferably two different shades as these are knitted in different directions and 50gm (2oz) will be needed altogether.

Four oblongs are made on 20sts for 42 rows, and four are made on 23sts for 39 rows. Sew these together to form an oblong 23cm (9in) deep and 40.5cm (16in) wide.

Measurements: each oblong, 11 × 10cm (4½ × 4in) and complete terrace, 40.5 × 23cm (16 × 9in).

Y. The lawn is knitted in two shades of green in g st, but there is no cast on edge. Instead, pick up 48sts from the left side of the terrace and work in alternate greens for 6 rows each. Do not break off the yarn at each change but twist it with the working yarn at the side to prevent a loop forming. Work 76 rows or until long enough.

Measurements: 23 × 20cm (9 × 8in).

Z. Two wide green borders on each side of the terrace almost wind up this alphabet of pieces! For the sake of unity, they should be in the same green as the other borders, but this is not essential.

Using DK yarn, cast on 32sts and work in double moss st for 37cm (14½in). With thicker chunky yarn, cast on 26sts, using 5mm needles.

Measurements: 37 × 15cm (14½ × 6in).

Assorted foliage

For (O), assorted green pom-pons for bushes. Tiny cabbages, see instructions on page 86.

For (P), a narrow strip of fur st in bright colours. 5 green pom-pons in a row. Border plants, flowers and foliage, see No 1 and 2 on page 91 for instructions.

For (Q), border plants, flowers and foliage, see No 3 and 4 on page 91 for instructions.

All other plants lower down the garden, except for the side borders, are represented with pom-pons in assorted colours.

Flowerpot boxes (K)

These applied pieces are pockets where little treasures may be kept safely, or hidden! Make 9 in each colour.

Materials required, about 2 × 50gm (2oz) balls DK yarn, one each in stone and brick-red. Size 4mm needles.

The same pattern is used for both colours.

Cast on 24sts.

Row 1: (k4, p1) 4 times, k4.

Row 2: (p4, k1) 4 times, p4.

Rep these 2 rows until 7 rows have been worked.

Row 8: knit.

Work 7 more rows as rows 1 and 2, then work in g st for 5 rows. Cast off.

Sewn underneath the herbaceous borders so that when they hang over the edges of the bed, they will look like flowerpots. Leave the top edges open.

Above: Close-up showing part of the vegetable plot and the flower-pot pockets along the side edges of the bedspread.

Trellis (V)

Made in two pieces, one 53.5cm (21in) long, and the other 15cm (6in) long: the longer one has a free-swinging gate of double fabric. Both are 9cm (3½in) wide.

Materials required, about 50gm (2oz) of various greens and off-whites, or pale grey DK yarns, size 4mm needles.

The gateway side, on the left, looking down the

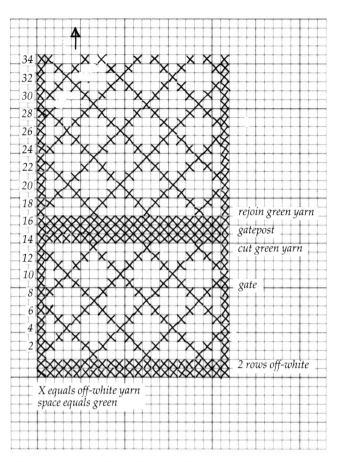

fig 2 **chart for trelliswork fence (V)**

Labels on chart:
rejoin green yarn
gatepost
cut green yarn
gate
2 rows off-white
X equals off-white yarn
space equals green

Above: A detail of the trellis, showing the gate unfastened.

garden. Using off-white yarn, cast on 22 sts and work 19 rows in pattern, see Fig 2, remembering to *knit* the first and last sts of *every row*. Break off the green yarn and knit the 20th row in off-white. This makes the fold at the edge of the gate.

Work 4 rows in ss in off-white, then rejoin the green yarn and work 13 rows of pattern.

Break off the green yarn again and work 3 rows of ss in off-white for the gate-post.

Join in the green yarn again and work in pattern for 121 more rows, (i.e 20 complete patterns from the gate-post). Cast off in off-white, weaving in the green yarn at the back as you go.

At the gate end, (the beginning), fold down the first 20 rows across the ridge and sew the edges together from the RS with off-white yarn. Sew the cast on edge.

The short side, on the right. Cast on 22sts in off-white and work 2 rows in ss for the gate-post. Now work in pattern for 34 more rows, remembering to *knit* the first and last sts in every row. Cast off in off-white, weaving in the end of the green yarn at the back.

These two pieces may need a gentle press. When sewing in place, leave the folded gate section to swing freely. Make two loops, one at each corner, and attach two large wooden beads to the opposite side, to keep the gate fastened down. For extra fun, sew a little

pocket into the underside of the gate as a place to keep a hanky or treat!

Crochet Afghan squares

For the small flower clumps (W).

Materials required, very small amounts of DK yarns, 3 colours for each square.

Begin with 4ch. Join these into a ring with a slip st.

Round 1: work into the centre of the ring, 5ch, (this counts as 1 treble + 2ch), 3tr, 2ch, 3tr, 2ch, 3tr, 2ch, 2tr. Join to 3rd ch of the first 5ch with a slip st. Fasten off.

Round 2: Join a new colour into one corner with a slip st then work 5ch, (to count as 1tr + 2ch as before), into same corner, work 3tr. For the side of the square work 1ch. For each corner, work 3tr, 2ch, 3tr. Rep this on each side and corner until you reach the last corner, where 2tr will now join the first tr of the 5ch where you began. Join with a slip st.

The brightly-coloured frill of chains is made by attaching a new yarn with a slip st to the first round and working loops of 6ch each on to the first and third st in each group, use a double crochet st to attach the 6th chain to the st.

For an alternative way to decorate this border, use coloured pom-pons of different sizes.

27

Dark green border

You may wish to omit the border shown on the outer edge of the bedspread, but I feel that it helps to enclose the bright colours and adds a finishing touch to the project. It is simple, although tedious to knit, but the length can be adjusted to fit your bedspread, as it is made in a narrow width from one corner to the next. Only three sides are bordered and the top, terrace end was left open. The diagram, see Fig 3, shows the working sequence, using garter stitch.

Materials required, about 8 × 50gm (2oz) balls of Chunky weight yarn. DK yarn *can* be used but this version was made in Chunky yarn on 5½mm needles for speed. If you use a finer yarn, be prepared to make more sections for each side.

For each side: cast on 16sts and k 20 rows.

Row 21: cast off 6sts and k to the end.

Knit 19 rows on these 10sts.

Cast on 6sts and k to the end.

Continue knitting in this way on 16 and 10sts alternately, always on the same edge of the border, until 13 sections are completed. To shape the corner, dec one st on the inner edge on every alt row until only one st rem. Finish off.

Make the other side in the same way.

For bottom edge: cast on one st and knit it.

Cast on one st on inner edge on next and alternate rows until there are 16sts. Now continue in the same way as the sides until 9 sections are completed. Commencing at the straight edge, shape the corner by decreasing as for the long sides.

Before finishing off the borders, check that you have knitted the correct length by temporarily pinning them on to your bedspread. Sew the mitred corners together, pin the borders in place and then oversew neatly all round. Press gently if necessary.

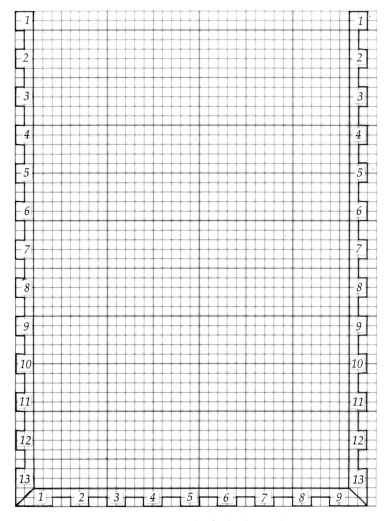

fig 3 **dark green border for bedspread**

House pillow, called 'Dove Cottage'

The pillow cover is made in five easy-to-handle sections. This allows the knitter to make adjustments to the sizing as work progresses, depending on the type of yarn used and the stitches chosen.

The brackets at the base of the large diagram indicate how the pillow cover is split into sections:–

First section; the LH window, door and roof, the centre chimney and sky.

Second section; the LH chimney stack and some green and blue background.

Third section; the RH side of the house with green or blue background.

Fourth section; the gable ends made in 2 narrow strips and sewn on. No instructions are given for this part.

Fifth section; (not shown on the diagram), is 7.5cm (3in) of double moss st in green DK yarn, to match the sides, in a long strip from one side of the base to the other.

All of these sections are sewn together with matching yarn. One square of the chart equals 2.5cm (1in).

Measurements

76 × 48cm (30 × 19in), or approximately 150sts and 114 rows!

Materials

These are only approximate estimates as the amounts will vary according to the yarns and stitches used and personal tension. DK yarns are used on 4mm needles.

Roof: 50gm (2oz) dark grey tweedy yarn.

Walls and chimney: 100gm (3oz) light grey tweedy yarn.

Windows: small amounts of charcoal grey and white.

Door: oddments of brown or any colour you prefer.

Background: 50gm (2oz) each pale blue and green.

Back of pillow: 200gm (7oz) green.

Stitches

The window and door details can be either knitted-in or Swiss-darned on top afterwards.

The walls, sky and fields are worked in plain ss, the chimney-stacks in moss st. The long strip of grass at the base is in double moss st, but no actual instructions are given for this; just begin at one end and continue until the piece is long enough, then cast off.

The two narrow strips to cover the gable ends of the house have shaped ends and are made in g st, but they can be made much more decorative than this by using a fancy edging st, or crochet, to resemble the

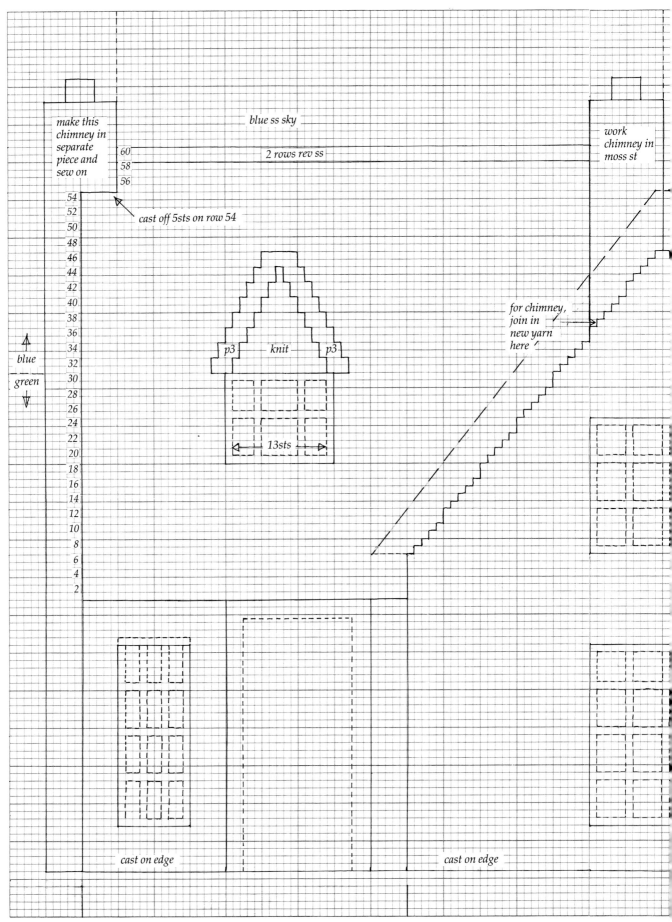

make this
chimney in
separate
piece and
sew on

blue ss sky

60
58
56

2 rows rev ss

work
chimney in
moss st

54
52
50

cast off 5sts on row 54

48
46
44
42
40
38
36
34
32
30
28
26
24
22
20
18
16
14
12
10
8
6
4
2

p3   knit   p3

13sts

blue

green

for chimney,
join in
new yarn
here

cast on edge

cast on edge

SECOND SECTION

FIRST SECTION

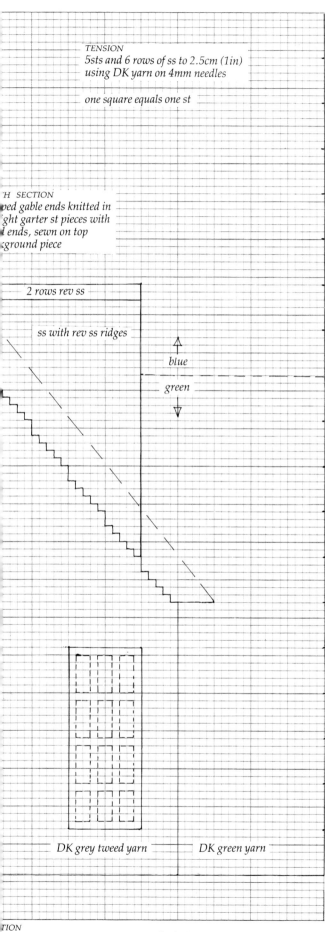

TENSION
*5sts and 6 rows of ss to 2.5cm (1in)
using DK yarn on 4mm needles*

one square equals one st

H SECTION
*ped gable ends knitted in
ght garter st pieces with
d ends, sewn on top
ground piece*

2 rows rev ss

ss with rev ss ridges

blue

green

DK grey tweed yarn — DK green yarn

TION

knitting chart for house pillow

decorative barge-boards of Victorian houses. These are often painted white.

The tile pattern for the roof is made over 6sts and 8 rows as follows:–

Rows 1 and 3: k5, p1 to the end of the row.

Row 2: k1, p5 to the end of the row, so that the k1 falls in the same place as the p1 of the previous row.

Row 4: knit, this makes a rev ss ridge on the RS.

Rows 5, 6, 7 and 8 are the same as the previous 4, except that the p1 now comes in the middle of the previous k5.

Just like tiles on a roof!

Making up

When all five sections are complete, carefully match the edges and join by oversewing from the WS. Press gently if necessary.

To make the back, cast on 150sts and work in double moss st until the piece is the same size as the front. If you prefer, make it instead from the narrow edge and pick up sts, working along to the other side. When sewing the two sides tog, remember to leave one narrow end open, crochet a border of loops down the two edges, make a long cord of matching yarn and lace this, like shoe laces, down to one corner.

Extra details

A. Pom-pons have been attached to the lower edge of the house to create foliage and an extra dimension.

B. The door-knocker and knob can be embroidered on.

C. The sunflower can be found on page 95. There is a three-dimensional variety too.

D. The dove on the roof can be found on page 113. Why not embroider a dove-cote at the side of the house?

E. Any of the people can inhabit the garden bedspread and Dove cottage, either the small ones or the larger Dove family.

plan of house pillow

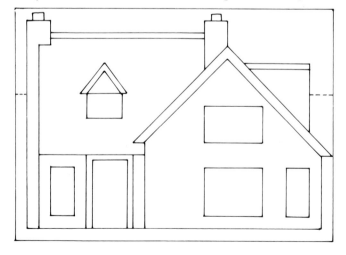

Seed packets

A delightful project for both knitters and embroiderers, and one of these very special seed packets translated into stitchery would make an ideal gift for a garden-lover. The fact that it still looks like the original seed packet rather than simply a picture of the plant lends even more charm to this idea, and the effort involved in this small-scale approach is well worth making.

In each case, the knitting or embroidery is set inside the actual packet. While specific instructions are not given for these pieces, (your own seed packet picture and your skills will decide which method you use), some helpful hints are listed here. Read through *both* lists before you decide. All four examples were made by Sandra Goode.

Knitted seed packet

1. The finer the yarn and needles you use, the more detail can be achieved. Throughout these examples, 2 ply crewel wool and DMC Broder Medici were used on 2mm needles.

2. Do not cut the square out of the packet until the knitting is complete as you may find that the fabric has contracted from its original measurements. For this reason also, cast on an extra border of stitches so that enough is available to tuck under the frame.
3. To decide which area, and what size to knit, cut a window from a piece of plain white paper. Make this window the size you intend to knit, and place it over the packet, holding it in position with paper clips when you have discovered the area to be worked. Use this as your guide until the work is quite finished, *then* the packet can be cut to the exact size.
4. Allow enough knitting to extend beyond all four edges of the packet frame. The knitting is then slid inside the packet behind the window frame and the square which you cut away will remind you of the original.
5. When the knitting is complete, darn all ends in securely to avoid tiny holes appearing.
6. It is quite acceptable to embroider extra details on top of your knitting when it is finished. Swiss darning is useful for adding extra details of colour, and the Cineraria has detached chain stitches which give a very realistic effect of texture.
7. Match all colours and tones very exactly in daylight.

This is improtant as it will show how well the knitting blends with the rest of the photograph from a distance. The wrong green will give the game away!

8. Use short lengths of coloured yarns along the row rather than weaving everything in behind.

9. When it is finished, press the piece *very gently* under a damp cloth. To mount it in the packet, carefully cut the packet open down the centre of the back and along the lower edge, then lay it out flat. Then place double-sided sticky-tape all round the window on the wrong side, (i.e the inside). Lay the knitting flat with the RS uppermost and place the window in position over the top so that the correct placing can clearly be seen. Press down firmly. The packet can then be folded back into its original shape and glued carefully together again. It is now ready for a frame. One of the clip-on varieties is best for this.

Canvas work seed packet

1. As with the knitted examples, the area covered with stitches extends beyond the cut-out window of the seed packet. Leave more canvas at the edges of your embroidery to avoid a gap showing.

2. This piece is small enough to be worked without an embroidery frame. The canvas used was single canvas of 18 holes to 2.5cm (1in), but double canvas may be used, finer if preferred.

3. Use single and double strands of any fine threads, crewel wools or cottons. The aim is to use anything which will give the effect you require, will pass through the eye of the blunt-ended needle and will not distort the canvas as it passes through.

4. The only stitch used here is tent stitch, (its other name is half cross stitch), but any other stitch may be included for extra effect. Experiment!.

5. No pre-design or working drawings were made, nor are they needed. Simply select colours with great care, don't be rushed into starting this exercise with the wrong ones. You'll regret it if you do!

6. Read the hints for the knitted version, there is some advice there which applied to embroidery also.

7. As tent stitch tends to distort canvas, blocking may be necessary.

Walled garden

This was intended as a wall hanging and measures 101.5 × 101.5cm (40 × 40in) and came about quite by chance. Having a large piece of free-style knit/crochet fabric left over from another project, I decided to cut it up into small squares and re-organise them into a colourful abstract patchwork. As it turned out, the effect was far less abstract than I had expected it to be and a garden began to form almost of its own accord. As one does in such circumstances, I let it develop in its pre-programmed way, as though I had little say in the matter. The exercise was rather like doing a textured jig-saw puzzle without knowing what the end result is supposed to look like. Great fun!

Spaces appeared between some of the textured squares which demanded plain low-key textures and paler colours as a contrast. These were manufactured in knitting and crochet, plain and fur stitches, swapping things around to adjust the balance, mostly working on the floor and standing on a chair so that I could get far enough away from it to judge the effect from a distance. It appeared to balance well from any angle without a definite top or bottom so it seemed sensible to border it in a way which made full use of this potential. A secret walled garden emerged, with openings on all four sides for quiet people to stroll into and meander among the foliage, to breathe in the scents of herbs and to feast the eyes and soul with the play of light and shade, colour and texture. This is one of the simplest designs I have ever made, and one of the most effective.

The size of the hanging was not decided until all the square units were arranged and the borders attached. Several types of units were used, free-style knit/crochet, (see note below), fur stitch in both knitting and crochet, both sides of stocking stitch and plain crochet trebles. A huge variety of yarns was used, all thicknesses, textures and colours, especially random-dyed yarns and several thicknesses used together.

The 10cm (4in) squares were sewn on to a background of heavy-duty, non-woven interfacing, by hand. To keep them in position during this process, the pieces were glued lightly on to the backing. The walls were made in a tweedy yarn to look like old stone. Each strip, eight in all, folds over the edge of the interfacing on to the reverse side, where it is sewn down. Square pieces were made for each corner and these also cover the reverse side. Padded knobs were sewn on to the sides of each opening and the whole is backed by more interfacing which contains a long pocket for the rod at the top.

Extra note: the free-style knit/crochet mentioned above is explained in great detail in 'Wool 'n Magic', by the same author and publisher.

'Crocus field' by Anne Coleman

The previous pages show how projects based on photographs of a highly textural nature can be translated into patterns of stitches where the edges of the latter match up exactly with the borders of the former. The small panel shown here is another version of the same idea, where a series of photographs of the same subject provide the setting for a piece of knitting. The knitting could have been placed at any point in the collage of photographs, foreground, middle distance or far distance and this is usually determined by the scale of the stitches which the artist can produce. The area farthest from the viewer would obviously require much finer stitches and a greater blending of colours than knitting on this scale could produce. The size of the panel was also determined by the size of the photographs and the scale of the subject: there is no rule about this except that one must be aware of proportions. *This* knitted panel is roughly one third the size of the surrounding material.

Another arrangement might be to use photographs, or one enlarged one, as a rectangular or circular frame for the knitted panel. Conversely, the photograph could be in the centre of the knitting. In the latter case, one would knit four borders which would fit together at the corners, or make a rectangle with a completely blank area in the centre where the photograph would be placed. The latter method would allow you to adjust measurements according to the finished size of the piece, in case of slight distortions.

In the left hand corner of the photograph, you will see a small sample of the yarns used by the artist in her knitting. This is a necessary part of the preparation for the project, as a wide variety of tones can be discovered by a careful visual search of the photograph and the mixture of these tones made by individual stitches is rather akin to the 'pointillist' technique of painting, where tiny dots of colour are mixed to achive a vibrant and lively effect.

If you can collate photographs of garden colours, textures, patterns and shapes, try this way of putting them together to build up a design. No drawing is needed, no charts or written instructions and no strict conformity to plan either. The edges of the knitting, unlike the previous exercises, do not exactly blend, but the scale of the knitted flowers and foliage is the same as those in the photographs, and the colours and tonal variations also match. Another point you will no doubt have noticed is that some of these photographs are duplicates which have been placed alongside each other to extend the area and some even overlap.

Cottage Row and gardens

THE COTTAGES

Walk through any village and you will see at least one group of cottages which look as though they have been there since the village began. Peep over the hedge or fence and see the owner busily tending the garden, tying up the beans, pottering in the lean-to or greenhouse, digging up a cabbage, or lean over the gate and pass the time of day.

Your knitted cottage can be based on reality or a dream: the ones here on Cottage Row may give you just a few ideas which you will be able to translate into your personal style, with all the details required to make it your own. The smallest figures will fit in here almost perfectly, though they may have to stoop a little to get through the doorways. You will find them on

Above: These three cottages are made to exactly the same pattern, but the use of colour and stitch patterns gives each one a uniquely different appearance.

page 98 but, meanwhile, make their homes and gardens.

The three cottages share exactly the same dimensions while the added details enable you to make each one quite individual. You can also choose whether to make them in foam or card, the only difference being that the card cottage has no base, thus having the advantage of one less piece of knitting to do and also providing a hollow cottage where things can be hidden. With a hinged roof, a cottage could also become a box. Both types have separate card roofs so that they can overhang on all sides.

A full description of the gardens is given on page 45.

Materials for the foam construction

1. Block of foam for each cottage measuring 15 × 13 × 7.5cm (6 × 5 × 3in).
2. Ruler, felt-tipped pen or marker, craft knife and scissors, adhesive tape.
3. Heavy mounting, or 'box' card, as follows:–
For the roof, 16.5 × 15cm (6½ × 6in).
For the dormer window, 8 × 7.5cm (3¼ × 3in).
For the chimney, 11.5 × 2.5cm (4½ × 1in).
For the porch, 14 × 2cm (5½ × ¾in).

Materials for the card construction

Piece of thick mounting card measuring 47 × 14cm (18½ × 5½in). This takes the place of the foam block needed for 3 cottages. You will also need some strong glue, see page 9.
Other requirements are the same as those listed in No 2 and 3 for the foam construction.

Material for the roof

The roof is made from card and is the same for both the foam and card constructions.
Cut a piece of strong card 15 × 7.5 × 7.5cm (6 × 3 × 3in). Score lightly along this to make a fold, see Fig 1e.
This piece will be covered with knitting and will fit on top of the cottage shape, so that the eaves overlap on all sides. *Do not glue in place at this stage.*

Foam construction

On each block of foam cut to the above measurements, mark a line all round 5cm (2in) from the top, as shown in Fig 1a opposite.
At each narrow end, mark diagonal lines from the centre to the sides, as shown at Fig 1b.
Mark the centre roof ridge as shown at Fig 1c.
Cut away two wedge-shapes at each side of the central ridge, using a sharp craft knife. The two pieces left over may be used to form the roof of another cottage

but in this event, you will need to cut an oblong of foam for the cottage block measuring 15 × 7.5 × 7.5cm (6 × 3 × 3in).

Card construction

Cut the card according to the diagram, see Fig 2a, then score and bend along the dotted lines. Turn the 1cm (½in) flap to the inside and glue to the nearest wall, noting that there is no base to this version. Cut and score the piece of card for the roof, see Fig 1e.

Dormer window

This is the same for the foam and card versions.
Using the diagram as a template to draw round, cut a piece of thick card to this shape and lightly score along the dotted lines. Bend the two wings backwards to meeet along the centre roof ridge, see Fig 2b.
Draw the window frames and shade in the window areas with paint or felt-tipped pens.
Fix the shape in place with adhesive tape but *do not fix to the roof yet.*

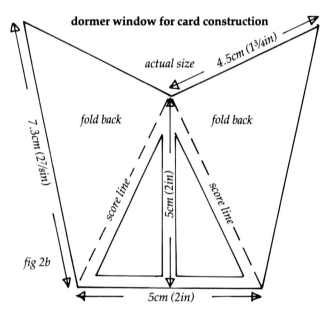

dormer window for card construction

actual size   4.5cm (1¾in)

7.3cm (2⅞in)

fold back   fold back

score line   5cm (2in)   score line

fig 2b

5cm (2in)

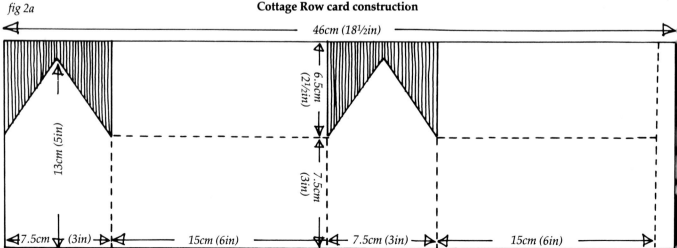

fig 2a   Cottage Row card construction

46cm (18½in)

6.5cm (2½in)

13cm (5in)

7.5cm (3in)

7.5cm (3in)   15cm (6in)   7.5cm (3in)   15cm (6in)

score along dotted lines: cut along solid lines remove shaded areas

1cm (½in)

38

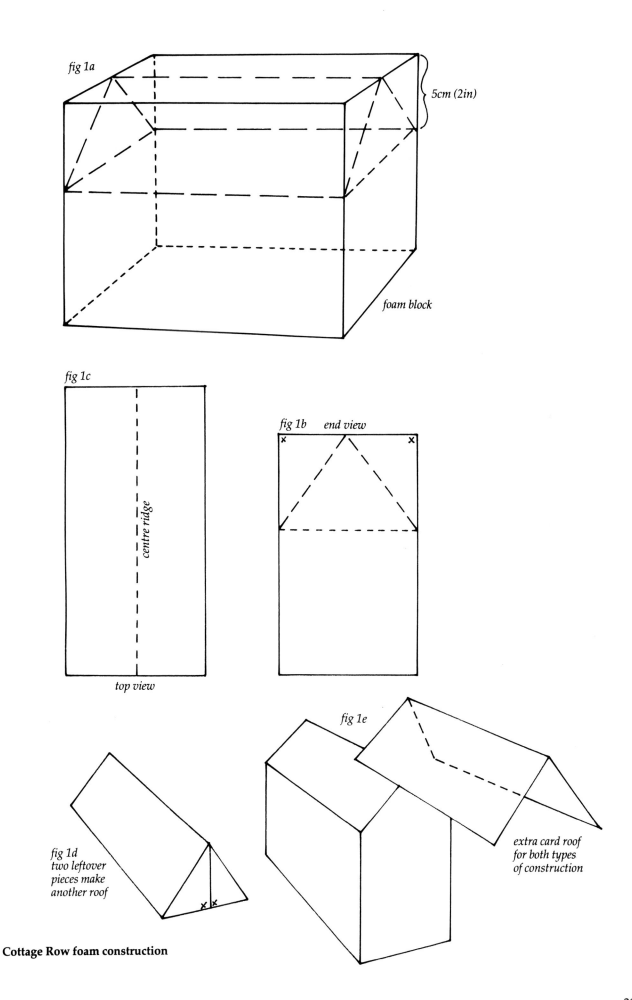

fig 1a

5cm (2in)

foam block

fig 1c

centre ridge

top view

fig 1b   end view

fig 1d
two leftover
pieces make
another roof

fig 1e

extra card roof
for both types
of construction

Cottage Row foam construction

Chimney

This is the same for the foam and card versions.
Using the diagram, see Fig 3a, as a template to draw
round, cut out the shape, remove the semi-circles and
score lightly along the dotted lines.
Fold the piece as shown, see Fig 3b, and glue the flap
on to one side. Bind all round with adhesive tape,
keeping the cut-out areas clear. *Do not glue to the roof
yet.*

showing the chimney

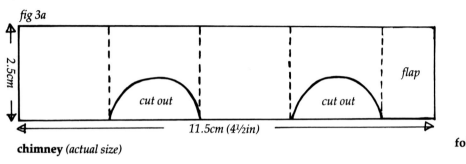

chimney *(actual size)*

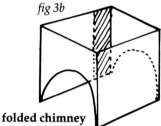

folded chimney

Porch

This is the same for the foam and card versions.
Cut a narrow piece of strong card as shown in the
diagram, see Fig 4, and score it along the dotted lines.
Bend the shape to form an archway but *do not* glue the
porch in place at this stage.

showing the porch

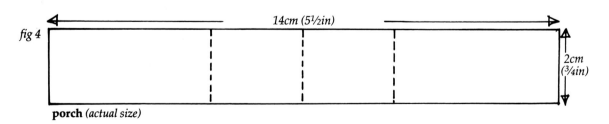

porch *(actual size)*

40

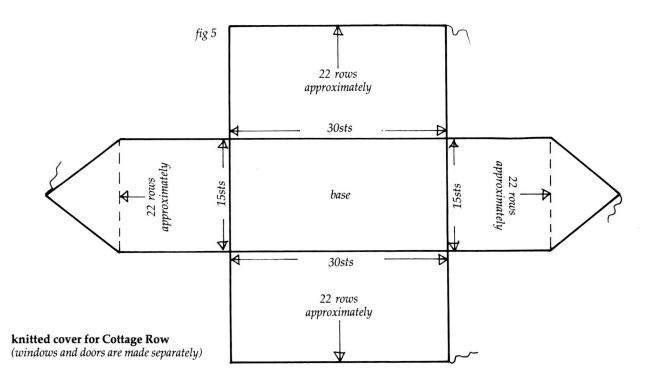

fig 5

22 rows approximately

30sts

22 rows approximately

15sts

22 rows approximately

base

15sts

22 rows approximately

30sts

22 rows approximately

knitted cover for Cottage Row
(windows and doors are made separately)

Sizes and materials for the knitted covers

All the pieces are made in DK yarn but as some tend to be thicker than others it is *essential* that you measure your knitting from time to time to check that it will fit the shapes.

Amounts needed are very small, only 25gm (1oz) for the four walls and the base. The roof takes almost 25gm (1oz), depending on the type of yarn. All other small features take only metres (yards) of oddments. The windows and door are made separately and sewn on afterwards. Use size 4mm needles thoughout, including the dormer, but for the windows you will need size 3¼mm needles to achieve a denser fabric.

Note: adjust the number of stitches and rows according to the yarn used and your own personal tension. Check on measurements constantly.

Knitted covers

Basically, all three cottages are covered in the same way but minor variations are achieved by yarn and stitch pattern.

The card construction has no knitted base, so in this version the walls must be glued in place round the lower edge. You can choose either to make each wall separately, to knit the large walls and base all in one, or even knit all four walls in one continuous strip. The diagram, see Fig 5, is given here so that you can choose whichever is most convenient, though the instructions for each piece are given separately.

Base (foam construction only)

In your chosen yarn, cast on 30sts and work in ss for 22 rows. Cast off.

Long walls

Cast on 30sts and work in the stitch of your choice for 22 rows. Below are given three versions, one for a stone-block effect, one in rough sandstone and one smoother (whitewashed) stone.

Pattern 1: use a grey tweedy yarn and some white, for this stone-block pattern.

Begin with RS facing and using grey yarn, purl.

Leave grey yarn hanging, join in white yarn and k one row.

Row 1: (WS) With grey yarn, p2, (sl 1 p-wise, p5) 4 times, sl 1, p3.

Row 2: (RS) p3, (sl 1 k-wise, p5) 4 times, p2.

Row 3: k2, (sl 1 p-wise, k5) 4 times, sl 1, k3.

Row 4: as row 2.

Row 5: with white yarn, p across all sts.

Row 6: knit.

Row 7: with grey yarn, (p5, sl 1 p-wise) 4 times, p6.

Row 8: p6, (sl 1 k-wise, p5) 4 times.

Row 9: (k5, sl 1 p-wise) 4 times, k6.

Row 10: as row 8.

Rows 11 and 12: as rows 5 and 6.

Rep these 12 rows once more (24 rows), and then work rows 1 to 4 again. Using grey yarn, cast off k-wise.

Important note: this pattern requires more rows than ss because of the contracting effect of the slip st pattern, so this piece will not be too long for one wall.

Pattern 2: use a sand-coloured rough-textured DK yarn for this rough sandstone effect.

Cast on 30sts and work in rev ss for approximately 22 rows then cast off.

Pattern 3: use white DK yarn for a smoother whitewashed stone wall.

Cast on 30sts and work 4 rows in moss st. Keeping 4sts in moss st at each end of every row, work 18 rows of ss then cast off in moss st.

Short end walls

The shorter end walls of the cottages are shaped to a point at the top, so each pattern is set out below.

Pattern 1: cast on 15sts with grey yarn and knit one row. Join in white yarn, p one row, k the next. With grey yarn continue:-

Row 1: (WS) p4, sl 1 p-wise, p5, sl 1 p-wise, p4.
Row 2: p4, sl 1 k-wise, p5, sl 1 k-wise, p4.
Row 3: k4, sl 1 p-wise, k5, sl 1 p-wise, k4.
Row 4: as row 2.
Rows 5 and 6: with white yarn, p one row, k the next row.
Row 7: with grey yarn, p1, (sl 1 p-wise, p5) twice, sl 1 p-wise, p1.
Row 8: p1, (sl 1 k-wise, p5) twice, sl 1 k-wise, p1.
Row 9: k1, (sl 1 p-wise, k5) twice, sl 1 p-wise, k1.
Row 10: as row 8.
Rows 11 and 12: as rows 5 and 6.
Rep these 12 rows once more, then rows 1 to 4 again. Begin shaping for the pointed gable.
Row 1: with white yarn, p2tog, p11, p2tog.
Row 2: k13.
Row 3: change to grey yarn, p6, sl 1 p-wise, p6.
Row 4: p2tog, p4, sl 1 k-wise, p4, p2tog.
Row 5: k5, sl 1 p-wise, k5.
Row 6: p2tog, p3, sl 1 k-wise, p3, p2tog.
Row 7: with white yarn, p9.
Row 8: k9, cut white yarn and weave end in on next row.
Row 9: p2tog, p5, p2tog.
Row 10: p7.
Row 11: k2tog, k3, k2tog.
Row 12: p5.
Row 13: k2tog, k1, k2tog.
Row 14: p3.
Row 15: k3tog.
Leave a long end before cutting yarn.

Pattern 2: cast on 15sts and work in rev ss for approximately 22 rows, then shape the top by dec one st at each end of every k row until only 3sts rem. P the next row, then k3tog. Leave a long end before cutting the yarn.

Pattern 3: cast on 15sts and work 4 rows in moss st. Keeping 3sts in moss st at each end of the rows, work 18 rows of ss. Now shape the top:-

Row 23: k1, sl 1, k1, psso, k to last 3sts, k2tog, k1.
Row 24: k1, p to last st, k1.
Rep these 2 rows until 5sts rem after a p row.
Next row: k2tog, k1, k2tog.
Next row: k1, p1, k1.
Next row: k3tog.
Leave a long end before cutting yarn.

Roof cover

This is an oblong piece made to cover the card roof, which will be glued on top of the cottage once the knitted walls are in place. Two patterns are given, one slate and one thatched but as with all the other pieces, any stitch pattern and yarn can be used to extend the variations. The piece must be large enough to cover the roof and to fold slightly underneath the edges on all sides. Check measurements as you go along.

The dormer window roof is also knitted in the same yarn, and 25gm (1oz) should be enough for both.

Tile pattern: cast on 34sts. Knit one row, purl one row, then knit another row. This makes a ridge on the RS and a flap to be turned under the eaves.

Rows 1, 3 and 5: (WS) (p4, k1) to last 4sts, p4.
Rows 2, 4, 6, 7 and 8: knit.
Work this patt twice more, then rows 1 to 7 again.
Centre roof ridge:—
Row 1: (RS) k2, (y fwd, k2tog) to last 2sts, k2.
Row 2: p34.
Row 3: p34.
Row 4: p2, (yrn, p2tog) to last 2sts, p2.
Row 5: p34.
Next row: (WS) begin tile patt again at row 1 and work as for the first side, finishing on row 8.
Complete the piece by working 2 rows of ss. Cast off.

Thatch pattern: the thatched roof is padded with a single, (not too thick), layer of synthetic wadding, or similar material. Cut this to exactly the same size as the card roof then glue the padding to the card. Trim the edges and allow it to dry while you prepare the thatch!
Cast on 40sts, (more than the tile pattern to allow for the padding), and knit one row, purl the second and third rows. This is the flap that turns under the eaves.
Now work 4 rows of single rib.
Row 8: knit.
Continue in single rib for 15 more rows.
Row 24: (RS) purl.
Row 25: knit.
Now work 4 rows of double moss st.
Row 30: p.
Row 31: k.
Rep the last 6 rows once again. This makes the patterned roof-ridge. Now continue in single rib for 15 rows.
Next row: (WS) knit, then work in rib for 4 rows.
Next row: (RS) purl, then purl the next row and knit the last one.
Cast off p-wise.

Dormer window cover

Using the same yarn as for the roof, cast on 23sts and knit 4 rows, noting that this is the same for all of the cottages.
Row 5: p2tog, p19, p2tog.

Above: Detail showing the dormer window and chimney in position.

Continue to decrease at both ends of every row until 3sts rem.

Last row: p3tog.

Leave a long end for sewing.

Chimney cover

Using the same yarn as for the walls, cast on 22sts and knit 8 rows, noting that this is the same for all of the cottages.

Next row: cast off 5sts, k5, (i.e 6sts left on RH needle), cast off next 5sts, k5, (i.e 6sts left in this group also). On each group separately, knit 4 rows, then cast off. Leave ends long enough for sewing.

Porch cover

Cast on 30sts and knit 6 rows, noting that this is the same for all of the cottages. Cast off.

Door inside porch

Using size 3¼mm needles, cast on 8 to 10sts. Knit one row then work in single rib for 16 rows. Cast off.
As the cast off end will round into the angled top of the porch, shaping is not essential. Embroider a door knob with a French knot or use a large round bead.

Windows and door

These are made separately so that you can choose where to place them once the cottage has been assembled. The charts, see Fig 6, show the patterns. Use size 3¼mm needles and DK yarns.

Window boxes

Use small oddments of brown and brightly-coloured yarns on size 3¼mm needles. With brown yarn, cast on 10sts and knit 2 rows. Change to green yarn and knit one row. Work one row in single rib, then cast off. Embroider the green strip with coloured French knots to resemble flowers, or use tiny beads and sequins.
For the larger dormer window-box, 16sts are needed.

Doorstep for cottage without porch

Use 3¾mm needles and DK yarn, cast on 9sts and work 5 rows in ss.

Row 6: knit.

Work 5 more rows in ss and cast off p-wise. Fold across the central ridge of rev ss and sew the edges together. Sew this to the base of the door.

Making up

None of the knitted pieces need pressing.

1. Assemble the main cottage pieces in position and sew up according to the diagram, see Fig 5 on page 41. For walls made in the stone-block pattern, match the corners so that the stones are aligned, carefully tucking in the white floating strands on to the inside.

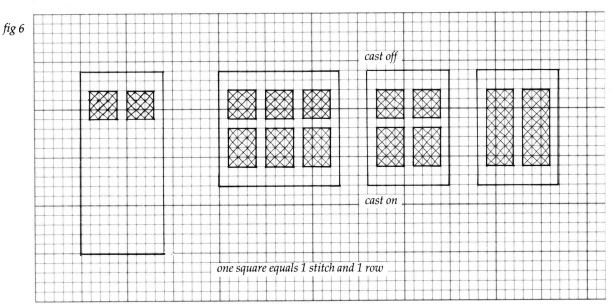

Door (left) and 3 windows (right)

2. Fit the walls and base on to the foam, (or card), foundation and pull the knitting level with all edges. Tie the points of the gables across the top as shown, see Fig 7, and lace across the ridge from side to side to keep the edges in place. Do not pull the yarn too tightly.

fig 7

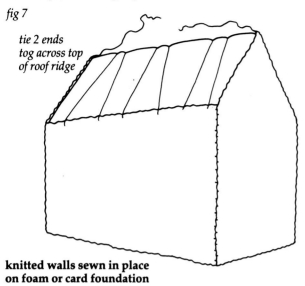

tie 2 ends tog across top of roof ridge

knitted walls sewn in place on foam or card foundation

If there is no base to your cottage, place a narrow line of glue round the card and stick the knitting to this. Glue can then be placed along the pointed ends and along the tops of the walls. Press the knitting accurately into place.

3. Tiled roof. Place the card roof in position on the knitted roof cover making sure that the roof-ridges lie in the same direction. Place glue along the longer edges of the card, on the *inside* of the card and fold over the three rows of knitting with the rev ss ridge on the edge. Allow 2 or 3 sts of knitting to project on each selvedge side.

   Now place a line of glue along each side of the card, on the inside again, and fold in the 2 side edges of knitting. Hold firmly in place until dry. One or two sts may be needed in each corner to hold them neatly.

4. Thatched roof, with extra padding. Fix the 2 long edges as for the tiled version. For the sides, lace across from one side to the other with yarn, pulling just enough to hold the edges well over on to the inside and conceal the padding. Fasten off securely and neaten the corners with a few hidden stitches if necessary.

5. Place the completed roof in position on the cottage and fix in place by glueing round the top of all knitted walls. Tuck all knitting well in so that no card or foam shows, allowing the roof to project slightly.

6. Dormer window. Cover the 2 roof sides of card with glue and lay the knitted piece over this, keeping the card well covered and allowing the front edges to roll over slightly on to the window frame. Pull the 2 points well down just free of the card as these will be sewn on to the roof.

7. Place the dormer window in position on the roof so that the lower window-sill is about 3 rows above the edge of the knitting. Sew the piece all round with matching yarn so that no stitches show.

8. Chimney. The 2 cut-out areas on the card-shape fit over the ridge of the roof. Glue the card chimney in position on top of the knitted roof, (i.e before fixing the cover on to it).

9. Sew the side edges of the knitted chimney-cover so that a tube is formed, taking care to allow for the different lengths of the 2 edges.

10. Either gather the edges of the top of the chimney-cover to close over completely or cut a small square of card and glue this just inside the top.

11. Glue just inside the edge of the card chimney and slip the cover over, pressing the top edges down inside by about 2 rows.

12. Pin the cover in place, pulling the 2 extensions well down on to the roof, and sew in place neatly all round.

13. Windows and doors. Decide where you will position these and either sew or glue them in place, but the door with the porch must wait until the porch is in place.

14. Glue the knitted porch-cover to the card-shape and, when dry, embroider plants and creepers on to this. Bend into shape and sew, or glue, to the wall of the cottage. The door can then be glued on to the wall inside.

15. Window-boxes can be sewn or glued in place.

THE GARDENS

Each little cottage has its own garden plot, all made to the same plan but each one different. The diagram, see Fig 1, shows the design but how you interpret it will depend on your own ideas and choice of colours, yarns and stitches. This is a 'mix 'n match' community, so when the cottage owners need a change, they simply swap plots, turn themselves round the other way, reverse their gardens and move their walls and hedges. Then, with the quick transplant of a few bushes here and there, the change is complete!

On the diagram, see Fig 2, the solid lines show changes of colour but this is for you to choose. All the garden plots shown in the photographs have been knitted to the same plan and only the colours and stitches have been changed. It is important to remember that numbers of stitches and rows will have

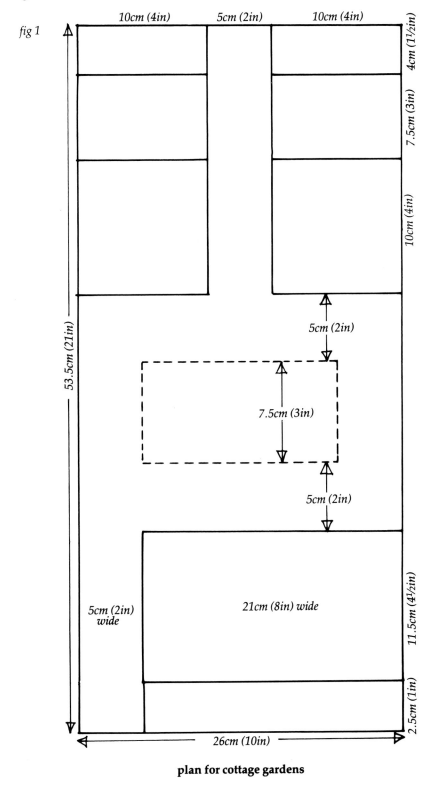

plan for cottage gardens

to be adjusted slightly as you go along, depending on the yarns and stitches used.

Measurements

Each knitted garden has been glued on to a piece of card measuring 53.5 × 25.5cm (21 × 10in). This helps to keep everything level and is easier to adjust and store.

Materials

The largest amount needed is for the central area and pathways, for which 50gm (2oz) should be allowed. All other areas can use up any small oddments available, estimating a total of roughly 125gm (5oz) of DK yarns. Size 4mm needles were used throughout.

Construction

Choose whether to make each piece separately and join them together afterwards, or knit the whole piece in one go. I made my version in a combination of both methods. Beginning at the top of the plan, I made the two side pieces separately, on 20sts each, then the pathway on 10sts, then joined them on to the same needle to begin the 16 rows of moss stitch, see Fig 2. From then on, the work was knitted in one piece down to the bottom.

Pond

This is simply a change of colour on the ss area in the centre of the paving, where two of the cottages stand. Use any dark blue and grey yarns together with a sparkling metallic yarn, and knit lilies to float on top. The top part of the fountain could also stand in it too, for instructions see page 74. The border round the edge can be made from along narrow strip of knitting or crochet.

Pink brickwork pathways

These are shown under the thatched cottage and for this pattern cast on a multiple of 6sts.
Rows 1 and 7: knit.
Rows 2 and 8: purl.
Rows 3 and 5: (k1, p4, k1) to end.
Rows 4 and 6: (p1, k4, p1) to end.
Rows 9 and 11: (p2, k2, p2) to end.
Rows 10 and 12: (k2, p2, k2) to end.
Cast off.

Extra details

All hedges, walls and fences can be found in chapter two, and there you will also find the greenhouse, cold frame, cloches, garden bench and other necessities with which to complete the cottage gardens. Choose any of the plants from chapter three and fill your garden with flowers, shrubs, trees and vegetables.

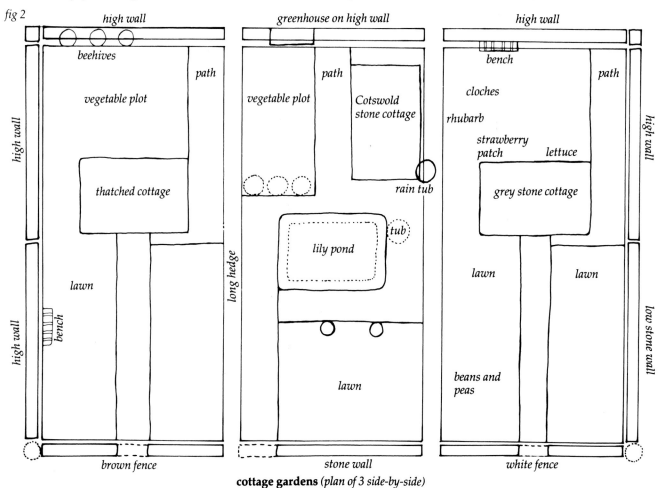

fig 2

cottage gardens *(plan of 3 side-by-side)*

PATCHWORK GARDEN EXTENSION

This garden extension is made entirely from 7.5cm (3in) squares in a mixture of the following:–

A. Knitted ss, both sides.
B. Diagonal g st.
C. Straight g st.
D. 2 and 3 colours to suggest plants, see page 90.
E. Knit/crochet free-style mixture, explained fully in 'Wool 'n Magic'.
F. Crochet, any textured stitch.
G. Canvas work, working any stitch with DK yarn on single or double canvas, mesh size about 10 to 12 holes to 2.5cm (1in). Leave a bare edge of about 8 holes all round the worked area and sew the edges of the adjoining knitted pieces on to this, close up to the stitchery. Outer edges of canvas work pieces are turned under and stitched down.

Materials

All pieces are made in oddments of green, neutral, stone and brown DK yarns, some smooth and some textured. Embroidery threads may also be used on the canvas, but this is not essential. Smooth knitting yarns will do just as well, but be sure to use a blunt-ended tapestry needle for this.

Patchwork pieces

To check that all squares are made to the same size, cut a piece of firm card exactly 7.5cm (3in) square and make all pieces to this size. The number of stitches you cast on will depend on the type of yarn used, but the needles should be size 4mm and hooks size 4.00mm. Try to arrange the squares so that the colours and textures are well balanced. Neutral and stone colours are useful to have near the edges, as these can then lead on into the cottage gardens and terraced areas as an extension. All pieces are sewn together. Use Swiss darning, (duplicate stitch), to cover up any ugly areas, edges, gaps or joins after sewing is completed, see page 119.

It should be pointed out that patchwork squares in mixed media have other uses too. With or without the canvas work, you can use them for garments, cushion covers, bedspreads and rugs or wall hangings. Make a garden bag in this way, or a foot mat for a dear friend's bedside, so that bare feet can still go into the grarden even in the middle of winter!

Border

To add a border at each end, perhaps to make up the exact length required, pick up stitches along the edge with a knitting needle, or crochet hook, and work on. Check your tension on one of your squares to see how many stitches per cm (in) you need, place pins along the edges as markers and allow these to guide you to obtain the correct number of rows. Garter or moss stitches are best for borders, as they lie flat without curling.

Friary garden, past and present

Many centuries ago, this ancient plot was contained within the grounds of a friary where the gentle Franciscans lived in peace and harmony with nature, tending the fruit trees, the vegetables and the flowers and caring for the friendly animals who came to visit. The friars kept bees for honey, used as a sweetener as there was no sugar at that time, and all the year round their labours produced food for the friary and a place of beauty for each other. Eventually, after some years of drought, bad winters and raids from the northern tribes, the friary came into the hands of the Dove family. It is their descendants who care for it now every bit as lovingly and still know it as 'the friary garden'.

Measurements

As with all the other projects, it is made in separate units which can be turned about in any direction to suit your own ideas. You can also choose whether the Franciscan friars still live there, or the modern Dove family. The three separate sections are shown on the diagram, see Fig 1, by double lines; these pieces are all of the same width but of different lengths. You can extend it in any direction or make it smaller, border it with topiary, pathways or herbs. Ideas for elaboration and extension are almost limitless; only time calls a halt! Look through the other chapters for the vegetables, garden furniture, trees and people. Measurements will be found on the diagram.

Materials

Amounts for the centre wall/hedge and archway are given separately.

For the vegetable plot and green garden, approximately 400gm (14oz) of DK yarn in assorted greens, browns and stones. All plants and accessories can be found in the seed catalogue and garden centre, or in the section on garden creatures. Both these main pieces were knitted on size 4mm needles.

Card pieces for mounting the sections are optional, but it does help to keep things flat and easy to handle. The size of these pieces is not of the utmost importance; just keep going until you run out of steam!

Vegetable plot

As you will note on the diagram, see Fig 1, this is made from strips of different widths which represent soil plots, and stone and grass pathways. For the

pathways, cast on about 16sts and knit in any stitch until the piece reaches the other end. Then join it to the next one and make another strip.

If this is to be a group project, it is always a good idea to draw a plan of the actual-size garden on brown paper, then take a copy of this, number all pieces on both original and copy, then cut up the copy to give to those who will be knitting the pieces. In this way you can be sure that all pieces will fit, no matter who makes them. A crochet or knitted border will ensure that all edges are neat and tidy when all sewing-up is complete.

fig 1 **friary garden**

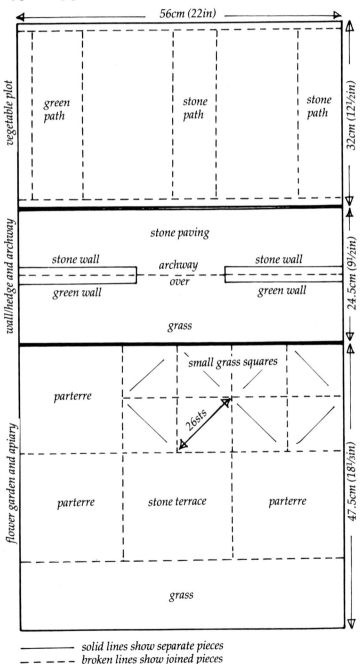

——————— *solid lines show separate pieces*
– – – – – *broken lines show joined pieces*

Opposite: Creatures from the fields and forest add to the activity in the friary garden.

Green garden

You will no doubt recognise three 'left overs' from the garden rug being used here in the green garden, along with the other small units. A stone terrace fits between two of them, making a useful area for the archway or the fountain to stand on. The green lawn is a patchwork of eight diagonal squares worked in g st, in oddments of greens, each of them 26sts across the widest part.

At the lower end, the darker green strip has been crocheted to the edge of the knitting but this can just as easily be done in knitting if you prefer. It can even be knitted lengthways and sewn on.

Centre wall or hedge and archway

This is a two-way construction with a stone wall on one side and yew hedge on the other. The archway in the centre divides the two sections of the garden (i.e the vegetable plot and the green garden). The coverings for each side are knitted in *double* DK yarn and thick needles for speed, but they can also be crocheted for even more speed! The measurements will be seen on the diagram, see Fig 2.

Materials for the card frame

1. Two large pieces of thick card measuring 56 × 35.5cm (22 × 14in). These are for the upright

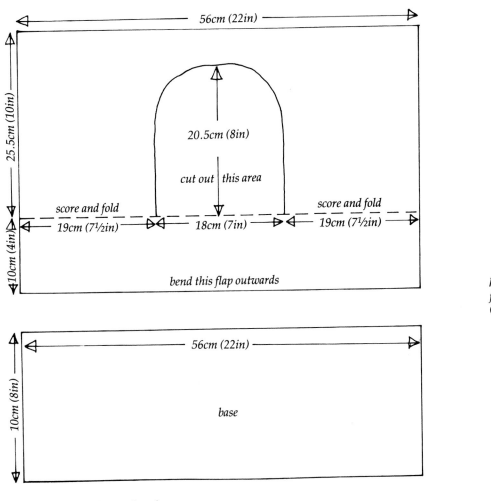

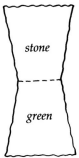

knitted keystone for centre of arch (not to scale)

fig 2 **wall/hedge and archway**

Opposite: The modern garden is carefully tended by the Dove family.

pieces and flap which stand together back to back. Another piece is needed for the base, measuring 56 × 20.5cm (22 × 8in).

2. Trace the arch-shape on to a piece of tracing or greaseproof paper and cut it out.
3. Measure the position of the arch on the card according to the diagram, see Fig 2, lay the cut-out tracing in position and draw round it. Now cut out the card archway using a sharp craft knife.
4. Score along the dotted line as shown and bend this outwards to lie flat.
5. Repeat this on the second piece of card, then lay the two pieces back to back and glue them together with the base flaps lying in opposite directions.
6. To stabilise the wall/hedge, glue both flaps down flat on to the card base.

Knitted cover

Each side is knitted in two halves, making a join above the arch which is covered by the keystone.

Materials: for the hedge side, 100gm (4oz) dark green DK, for the wall side, 100gm (4oz) stone DK, both used double. Sizes 6mm and 4mm needles

1. Using double stone-coloured yarn and size 6mm needles, cast on 28sts. The stitch used is basically the same as double moss st, except that 4sts and 4 rows are worked instead of two. Work 32 rows. Now make the top curve of the arch as follows:–
   Row 33: inc in first st, k3, continue in patt to end.
   Row 34: patt to last st, k1.
   Continue to inc at beg of alt rows, incorporating the extra sts into the patt at the end of the rows, until 12 more rows have been worked, (35sts).
   Next row: cast on 4sts and work in patt to end.
   Continue on these 39sts for 6 more rows, then cast off. Make another piece in the same way.
2. Using double dark green yarn and the same needles, cast on 28sts and work the same shape as for the wall side, but use double moss st *as normal*.

Make two pieces the same.

3. Stitch the two sections of each side together to form an arch, one stone and one hedge side.
4. With RS facing, lay the two pieces tog and pin. Stitch up the side edges and the top edge but leave the arch and base open.
5. Fold the piece to the RS and fit over the card frame.
6. Pin the two pieces of knitting together round the archway and sew neatly from the RS, using the flat seam.
7. Make the keystone for the centre of the archway as follows:– using *single* stone-coloured yarn and size 4mm needles, cast on 13sts and work 6 rows in single moss st. Now inc one st at each end of next and every foll 4th row, incorporating each new pair of sts into the patt until there are 19sts, (i.e 15 rows). Work 3 more rows.
   Next row: (RS) purl.
   Next row: change to dark green yarn and p one row.
   Next row: purl, then work 3 more rows in moss st. Now dec one st at each end of next and every 4th row until there are 13sts.
   Work 6 rows without shaping. Cast off.
8. Fold this piece over the centre of the arch, matching the colours, and sew the narrow ends together. Position the piece exactly in the centre of the arch then gently stitch the piece down on to the knitting beneath.
9. The cover for the flat base can be made in two separate strips of knitting or crochet. It can resemble cobblestones, or grass or soil, so choose the yarn accordingly. Using DK yarn and size 4mm needles, cast on about 24sts, knit or crochet the required length and glue the pieces in position on the base. Stitch them together neatly underneath the arch.
10. The walls and hedge can now be stitched along the bottom edges to the base on each side.

Building up your garden

Having chosen your garden plot, size and shape,
you must now stamp it with your own personality.
According to the materials available, decide on boundary
walls or hedges; what type of trees you prefer;
the positions of the flower and vegetable gardens
and the accessories which will bring it all to life.
Some of the box-shaped items, such as the greenhouse,
make excellent gift boxes.

Garden walls and fences

GARDEN WALLS
Cottage gardens

Part of the charm of many old-world cottage gardens is the high wall which encloses the patchwork of neatly tended fruit and flower beds, or the vegetable plots, sheltering them from cold winds and reflecting the light and warm rays of the sun. The latter depends upon the wall being whitewashed for maximum effect. If the red brick or grey stone wall is what you require, or even a sandstone one to take advantage of local materials, make sure you have enough of the same yarn which was used to make your cottage left over. It is quite likely that all the pathways will be in the same material too.

Measurements

These walls are 10cm (4in) high, just high enough for the lean-to greenhouse, which is 26cm (10in) long, and to coincide with the width of the cottage gardens. They can, of course, be made to any length you require.
The knitted cover fits over a foundation of card and can be as plain or as textured as you wish. Basically, it is a large oblong folded across the top with strips of coloured knitting at each end to cover the base.

Materials

50gm (2oz) of DK yarn in the chosen wall colour and small amounts of DK yarns for the base strips, in brown or green. Size 4mm needles.
Strong card for the foundation, see measurements below. Strong glue.

Card construction

Cut 2 pieces of card, each measuring 26 × 14cm (10 × 5½in), or slightly deeper if a wider base is needed. These are scored and bent as shown in the diagram, see Fig 1. Strong glue or a stapler will be needed. Score the cards along the dotted lines and bend them into L-shapes. Either staple or glue the 2 pieces back to back. To make the shape even stronger, another piece of card glued along the bottom helps.

Knitted pink brick wall

This has one patterned side and one plain side. Using dark brown or green for the base, cast on 52sts. This may be grass or soil, so use any appropriate stitch. The number of rows will depend on the stitch you have chosen, so measure it against the card for accuracy.
Change to wall-coloured yarn and work in double moss stitch for 24 to 26 rows, or in ss for 22 rows. Then work 2 knit rows to begin the decorative edging at the top.
Row 29: (i.e from the base of the wall), (k3, p2) to the last 2sts, k2.
Row 30: p2, (k2, p3) to the end.
Repeat these 2 rows once more.
Rows 33, 36, 37, 40 and 41: purl.
Rows 34, 35, 38, 39 and 42: knit.
Rep rows 29 to 32.
Rows 47 and 48: purl.

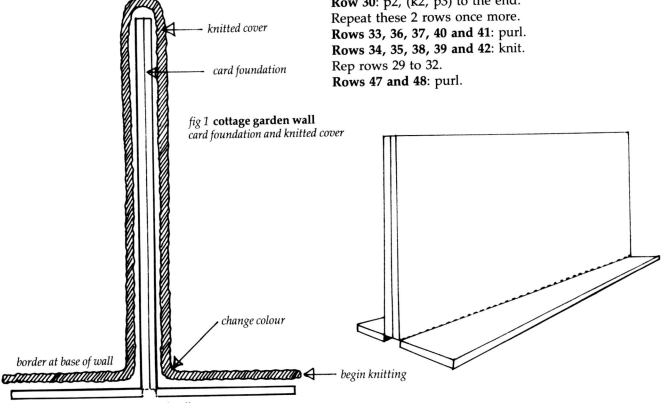

knitted cover

card foundation

fig 1 **cottage garden wall**
card foundation and knitted cover

change colour

border at base of wall

begin knitting

end section of wall

Row 49: (RS facing) cont in ss for 22 rows or for 26 rows in double moss st.

Now change back to border colour and work as before until this piece reaches the edge of the card base. Cast off.

Making up

Pin and sew up the two side edges of the wall: the borders are left free. Slip the cover on to the card foundation, glue along the card base, (not the wall), and press the knitted border on to this at each side. Pull well forward to cover all edges and corners, see Fig 1.

Whitewashed wall

This has a wide border of grey tweedy yarn for the greenhouse to stand on. The border measures 5cm (2in) wide, working about 14 rows of rev ss. Off-white tweedy yarn was used for the walls and the stitch is 3 rows of ss followed by one row of k1, p1. This is, in effect, like moss st separated by 3 rows of ss. Continue in this st until 9cm (3½in) have been worked. Now make the coping-stones for the top:–

Next row: (RS facing) p one row.

Now work 4 rows of k2, p2 rib.

Next row: knit, noting that this is the top edge of the wall.

Continue with 4 rows of k2, p2 rib, then one p row. Begin the wall pattern again and continue for 9cm (3½in). Finish off the border in the same way as the other side. The espalier fruit trees growing against this wall can be found on page 84.

Corner pieces

As gaps may be formed in the corners when large walls are placed together, corner pieces help to solve the problem. Make the knitted covers to match the walls or make the four sections of the knitted cover in different colours so that corner can be turned round to match any wall.

Corner piece card foundation

1. Cut five pieces of strong card as shown in the diagram, see Fig 2.
2. Mark each piece with solid and dotted lines as shown.
3. On each one, cut out the shaded area, two from the left and two from the right corners.

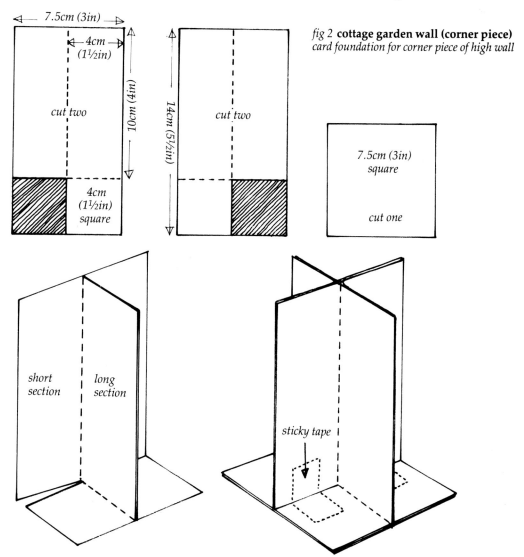

fig 2 **cottage garden wall (corner piece)**
card foundation for corner piece of high wall

Note: it does not matter if the scoring is done from the 'wrong' side as they will fit just the same, though not exactly as shown in the diagram.

4. Now score lightly along the dotted lines and fold the sections backwards to form the corner pieces.
5. Take 2 pieces with the opposite corners removed and place them back to back as shown in the diagram. Do the same with the other pair.
6. Staple, glue or use sticky-tape to hold these firmly in position.
7. Place these two pieces back to back, pushing the four shorter sides firmly together. Staple or glue as before.
8. This should now be glued firmly on to the square card base to hold all sections in position. A little extra sticky-tape will help to keep the 2 shorter sides down. It is now ready for the cover.

Knitted cover for the corner piece

Each cover is made in four separate sections.
Materials needed are small oddments of DK yarns left over from the high walls. Size 4mm needles. Glue.

1. Begin at the base, making a small square:– using green, brown or grey yarn, cast on 8sts and work in single moss st for 12 rows. On the 13th row, cast on 8sts and continue in moss st to the end of the row, (16sts). Cut the yarn and join in the wall colour. Using the same stitch as the wall, work in the same way to the top and cast off.
2. Make 3 more pieces in the same way.
3. Making up; fold up the small base squares to meet the lower edges of the walls and, with RS tog, sew up as shown in the diagram, see Fig 3.
4. With RS tog, pin all four pieces tog along the selvedges to form a tube, then sew. Place this piece over the card foundation so that all joins are on the outer edges of the walls, not in the corners.
5. Push each piece well into the corners and hold them together along the top edges with pins. This will form a cross following the shape of the card. These edges are now sewn together from the RS, see Fig 4.
6. Now remove the cover and glue both sides of the walls.
   Do not glue the base at this stage; you will need to hold this part.
7. Place the card foundation on the table and fit the cover over the top carefully, easing it into shape and adjusting the top edges first, then the outer edges, then the corners. Push on to the glue firmly, taking care to keep the knitting in shape.
8. Now glue each card base *one at a time* and ease each knitted base on to this, pushing back into the corners.

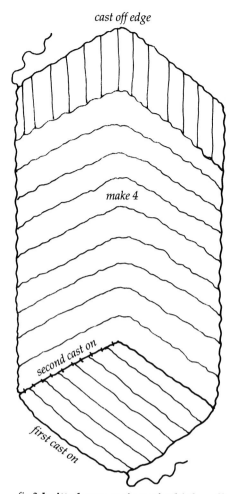

cast off edge

make 4

second cast on

first cast on

fig 3 **knitted corner pieces for high wall**

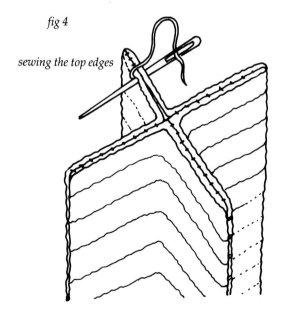

fig 4

sewing the top edges

GARDEN FENCES AND LOW WALL
Cottage gardens

These low boundaries can be made to any length, though several short ones are probably more useful than one long one. Make a variety to be used between the cottages as well as round the edges. They can also be used to separate different areas of the same garden.

The ones shown here are 25.5cm (10in) long and they stand 4cm (1½in) high. They are made over a foundation of strong card and, if you wish, can have a space in the centre to allow a pathway to pass through. The diagram, see Fig 1, shows how the card foundation is made; use staples, glue or sticky-tape to hold the two pieces of card together and stick the base on underneath for extra firmness, see Fig 2.

Materials

Two pieces of card measuring 25.5cm × 5cm (10in × 2in) and one measuring 25.5cm × 2.5cm (10in × 1in) for the base.
For the knitted covers; oddments of DK yarn in the chosen colours and size 4mm needles. Glue and staples.

Card foundation

To make the card foundation, mark the dotted lines on the card as shown in the diagram, see Fig 1, and score lightly. Fold back. Mark out the centre area if there is to be a pathway through and cut it out. Leave the base intact to hold the sides together.

Place the two pieces of card back to back with the narrow base folded outwards and glue and/or staple them in position. Glue the base in position on the underside.

Knitted covers for the stone walls

The wall is made in one piece, including the grass base. You will need oddments of grey/stone and greens.
Using green yarn, cast on 50sts and knit 3 rows. Change to stone yarn and knit one row. Now work 24 rows of double moss st. Change back to green yarn, purl one row then knit 3 more. Cast off.

Making up

1. With RStog, fold the piece in half along its length and sew up the stone sides leaving the green base free. Turn to the RS.
2. Glue both sides of the card wall and the upper base. Place the knitted cover over this and arrange carefully to fit exactly along the edges and base.
3. Press down and adjust the edges, pushing the green/stone fold into the bend of the wall.

Cotswold (sandstone) wall

This is made in one piece only 20cm (7¾in) long with a space at one end for the side pathway. The base is still 25.5cm (10in) long.

garden fences and low wall

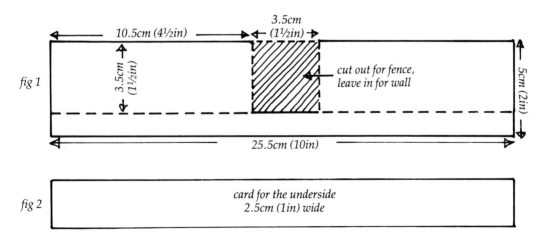

Knitted covers for the fences

Charts are given, see Figs 3 and 4, for both types of fences, worked on 28sts for each side of the central pathway. Knit two pieces for each complete fence. As for the stone wall, begin by knitting 3 rows of green g st for the base, then continue by following the pattern on the chart for either the white fence or the brown one. The small space in the centre of these two pieces is filled by a tiny square of moss st on 7sts worked for 9 rows. If you wish to change the colour of the pathway in the centre of your fence or wall after you have made it, knit a small square of the correct colour and glue it over the top.

Making up

1. Fold the 2 main pieces in half across the centres and sew up each end leaving the grass base free. Sew the small pathway between the 2 pieces on to the edges of the green base.
2. Glue the card fence and place the knitted covers over this, adjusting the edges and corners carefully before pressing into position. Pull the knitting gently to cover all parts of the card before the glue dries.

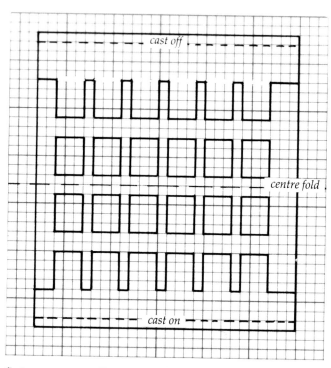

fig 3 **Brown wooden railings**

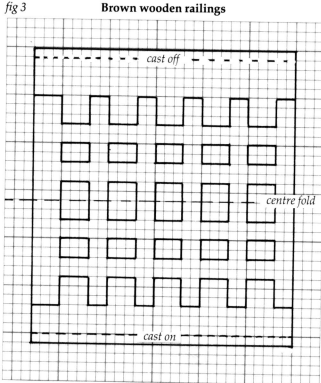

fig 4 **White painted fence**

FREE-STANDING ARCHWAY

Friary gardens

This archway can be positioned so that it leads the eye from one section of the garden to another.

Measurements

47 × 5cm (18½ × 2in).

Materials

Oddments of assorted DK yarns in green and white/stone. Size 4mm needles.
For the card foundation, a strip of bendy card of the above measurements and glue.

Knitted cover

The chart, see Fig 1, shows the pattern of the lattice effect worked on 15sts. Any assorted greens will do for this, as several different tones are more interesting than only one. The white yarn can also be varied.
Simply cast on 15sts and continue in pattern until the knitted strip is long enough to cover the card. If you wish, this strip can be continued in plain green ss to cover the inside of the archway, but this is not essential.
The knitted cover is glued on to the card, first the outside and then the inside, after which the two edges can be lightly stitched together all round. To keep the base firm, another piece of card may be glued across the bottom.

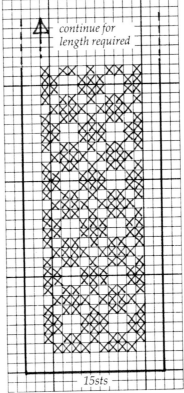

fig 1 **free-standing archway**
knitting chart for 2-colour pattern

continue for length required

15sts

X equals green
open space equals white

Greenhouses, cold frames and cloches

GREENHOUSE
Friary Gardens

Though the friars would probably not have had a greenhouse in the early years of their garden, the Doves would certainly find one useful to grow tomatoes, cucumbers, melons, grapes and flowers. This one is quite small, just big enough for John and his family to put their tenderest plants inside away from the cold night air.

It is a very simple construction and not at all difficult to make. It can also be adapted quite easily to become a tool shed, as the illustration on page 53 shows. No instructions have been given for the tool shed, however, just give it a try and keep notes as you go along. The greenhouse, (or tool shed), could also be adapted to become a box with a hinged lid, one which opens from one edge or down the centre roof-ridge. Imagine a keen gardener being delighted by a gift of a greenhouse box to keep her bisuits/tissues/seed-packets/knitting in! In this version, the door does not open, nor the windows, but these are refinements which could easily be built into the design if needed.

Only five pieces of knitting are needed, all rectangular, two of them with pointed tops. Even the colour-knitting is easy as the balls are kept separate to avoid stranding or weaving-in across the back. The knitting is based on a card foundation.

Measurements
26 × 21 × 16cm (10¼ × 8¼ × 6¼in).

Materials
Thick, strong card for the foundation. See the diagram, (Fig 1), for exact measurements.
Parcel tape and glue.
DK yarns in roughly the following quantities:–
20gm (¾oz) brown, 20gm (¾oz) white, 50gm (2oz) assorted greens, 50gm (2oz) pale blue 3 ply + Twilley's Goldfingering in silver *or* a DK pale blue alone.
Size 4mm needles.

Card foundation

Cut the card shape according to the diagram, see Fig 1, score along the dotted lines and fold up. Glue the flap at one edge and press this to the side wall to make a box. The sides and base can now be bound together firmly with parcel-tape. Do not fix the lid on at this stage, just score along the ridge and fold across to form a V-shape.

Knitted cover for long sides

Begin the knitting by making two long sides, both alike. Using brown yarn, cast on 52sts, ** and work 3 rows in ss beg with a k row.

Row 4: knit.

These first 3 rows will be turned under to the base of the greenhouse with the row of rev ss making a sharp edge all round.

Continue to work in ss, but make a ridge of rev ss, (as above), on every 5th row until 4 ridges in all have been made, about 6.5cm (2½in), ending on the last ridge row. Work one more rev ss row to finish (i.e a knit row) so that the next row can begin on the RS. Cut brown yarn, **.

Prepare the green and white yarns and cut 5 lengths of white yarn, each about 150cm (60in) long, and 4 lengths of green yarn, (all different), about 76cm (30in) long. Accuracy is not essential here. After being joined into the first row of the pattern, each length of yarn is left to hang in position at the back of the knitting to be picked up again when required on the next row, but to avoid gaps appearing between colours it is essential to twist each one with the one next to it by bringing the new yarn up from underneath the old one, see page 125. As each length of yarn is used up, simply tie on another different shade of green and knit through the

knot, weaving in the long loose ends on the back, or darn them in.

Work the window pattern as follows:–

Row 1: (RS) k3 white, (10 green, 2 white) 3 times, 10 green, 3 white.

Row 2: (WS) p3 white, (10 green, 2 white) 3 times, 10 green, 3 white.

Continue in ss in this patt until 26 window rows have been made. Now tie the first length of white yarn back on to the ball and work 2 rows of white ss across all sts, weaving in all other ends on the back.

Now make a ridge of rev ss to fold over the top of the side by p one row on the RS, then work another p row and cast off.

Knitted cover for narrow end wall

Make only one.

Using brown yarn, cast on 32sts and work as given for long sides from ** to **.

*** Prepare green and white yarns as before, but use only 4 lengths of white and 3 lengths of green. Work the window pattern as follows:–

Row 1: (RS) k3 white, 7 green, 2 white, 8 green, 2 white, 7 green, 3 white.

Row 2: (WS) p3 white, 7 green, 2 white, 8 green, 2 white, 7 green, 3 white.

Continue in ss in this patt until 26 rows of window pattern have been made, ***.

Now shape the top:– Work 2 rows in white across all sts, leaving all other lengths of yarn in place.

Next row: k2tog, patt to last 2sts, k2tog.

Next row: purl in patt.

Repeat these 2 rows once more, then the first row again. (26sts). Now continue to dec one st at each end of *every row* until only 2sts rem. K2tog and finish off.

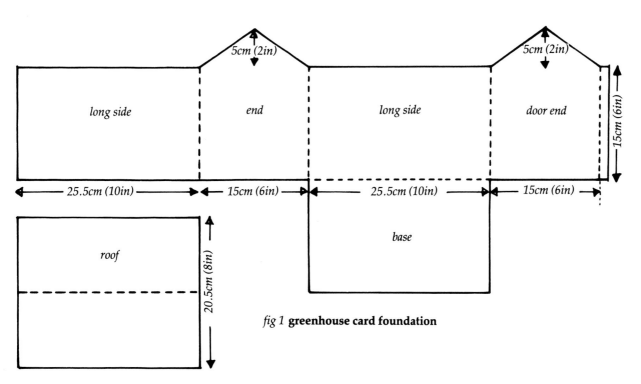

fig 1 **greenhouse card foundation**

Knitted cover for narrow wall with door

Make only one. Using brown yarn, cast on 32sts and work 3 rows in ss as before, followed by a knit row. Cut 2 lengths of white yarn as before and join these in on the next row to outline the door frame as follows:–

Row 5: k10 brown, 2 white, 8 brown, 2 white, 10 brown.

Row 6: purl in the same pattern.

Continue in this pattern, keeping the rev ss ridges as before on every 5th row, but at the sides only, not on the door or frame. As you approach the top of the brown section, make the last ridge across all sts except the white ones. Work one extra row as before so that the following row can begin on the RS.

Now continue as the other end of the greenhouse from *** to ***.

Shape the top as follows:–

Next row: k12 white, 8 green, 12 white.

Next row: p12 white, 8 green, 12 white.

Next row: k2tog, k1 white, 7 green, 2 white, 8 green, 2 white, 7 green, 1 white, k2tog.

Next row: purl in the same pattern.

Repeat these 2 rows once more, then the first row again, (26sts).

Next row: p2tog, p in patt to last 2 sts, p2tog.

Next row: k2tog, k4 green, 12 white, 4 green, k2tog.

Next row: p2tog, p3 green, 12 white, 3 green, p2tog.

Next row: k2tog, k2 green, 2 white, 8 green, 2 white, 2 green, k2tog.

Now continue to dec one st at each end of *every row* and keeping to the colour pattern as the last row above, finish the top as the other end.

Knitted cover for glass roof

This is made all in one piece with a ridge across the middle. Using white yarn, cast on 52sts. Beginning with a k row, work 3 rows in ss and knit the 4th to make a rev ss ridge which will fold underneath the edge of the roof. Work 2 more rows of ss.

Prepare 5 lengths of white yarn as for the long sides and use these with a continuous supply of pale blue and silver metallic thread or pale blue alone.

Row 7: k3 white, (10 blue, 2 white) 3 times, then 10 blue, 3 white.

Row 8: purl in the same pattern as above.

Repeat these 2 rows 12 more times, (26 rows of blue), taking care not to strand the blue yarn too tightly across the 2 white sts but allow it to lie fairly loosely to avoid contracting the knitting.

For the roof ridge, tie the first white length of yarn to the ball and leave all other threads in place, twisting them with the white yarn over the next 4 rows to move them upwards into position. Knit 4 completely white rows in g st.

Now continue in patt as before, making the second side match the first. Finish off with 3 rows all white, (weave the other ends in at this stage), and a 4th row of knit to make a ridge. Work 2 more rows of ss, then cast off.

Making up

A. Lay the four wall sections side by side in order, WS uppermost and pin together to form a tube. Sew each side up, using brown and white yarns, then turn to RS.

B. Slip the cover over the card box and position the corners. Turn the box on its side and run a brown gathering thread all round the cast on edge.

C. Before gathering up, place glue all the way round the underneath edge of the box roughly 1cm (½in) wide. Draw the gathering thread gently, readjust the corners and then press the first three rows of knitting on to the glue on the underside of the box. The first ridge of rev ss will now fit neatly on to the lower edges of the walls.

D. The top edges of the long walls are now to be glued in position: place glue along the *inside* edges at the top of the two long sides and turn the last few rows of knitting over on to the glue so that the ridge of rev ss lies along the top edge. Press down firmly and neaten the corners, taking care to adjust the position of the knitting before the glue dries.

E. Now place glue, one side at a time, on the outer top edges of the two narrow walls and press the shaped ends into place taking care to cover the card completely along the edges.

F. To complete the roof, place glue in a line along both long edges on the *underside* of the card. Fold the first and last few rows of knitting on to the glue, with the rev ss ridges on the extreme edges of the roof. Press in position neatly.

G. Lift the side pieces of knitting gently and place glue on the card beneath, all along the edges. Press the knitting into place, pulling the selvedges just a little way beyond the card at each side so that it overhangs.

H. Place glue all round the top edges of the walls on both knitting and card. Press the roof in place on to the walls, easing the ends into position under the knitting so that no gaps show.

I. Embroider the door knobs on the knitted door.

J. The two knobs on the gable ends are made by knitting a ss square of 8sts and 8 rows. Gather all round, pad and sew on, or glue.

Extra details

1. At some stage, either before making up or after, plants, flowers, pots and shelves can be Swiss-darned, (duplicate stitched), on to the windows.

2. The roof may be hinged on by sewing instead of glueing, to make the greenhouse into a box. You may also consider lining the box in some way, either with fabric, felt or knitting. If you do, make the sides fractionally smaller to fit inner dimensions. Alternatively, it could hinge on both edges and fasten along the central ridge.

3. The door can be made to open by knitting the end section in three pieces with an extra section made to fit above the door.

4. This greenhouse can easily be converted into a garden shed. Use the same dimensions but make the brown walls come higher up the sides and the windows placed centrally instead of from end to end. In the two narrow ends, no window is needed. The tools, pots and peat, watering can and other small items could be kept in here for safety when the garden is not in use.

SMALL LEAN-TO GREENHOUSE
Cottage gardens

This small version may also be used as a conservatory attached to one end of a cottage but here it is shown against the high white wall of a cottage, where the sun will reach it for most of the year. Used against the garden wall, glued or stitched into place, it will also help the wall to stand without the need for an extra base. A small door is knitted-in at one end, the door knob and flowers are embroidered on afterwards. It is knitted in one piece and mounted on a piece of shaped card. For measurements, see the diagram Fig 1.

fig 1 **small lean-to greenhouse**
diagram of card foundation

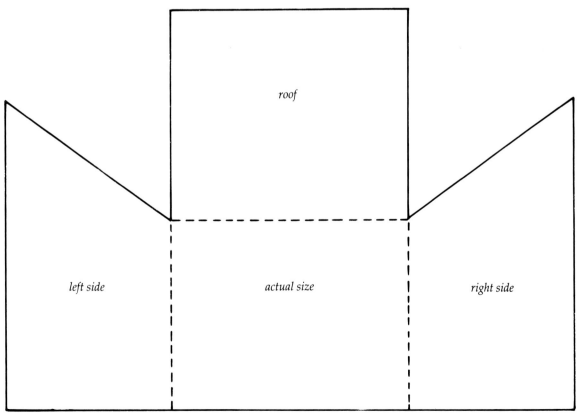

Materials

Small oddments of DK yarns in tones of green, a little pale blue and some white.

Size 3¼mm needles are used to keep the knitting more compact.

For the foundation, a piece of card measuring 16 × 12cm (6¼ × 4¼in). Cut this to the shape shown in the diagram. Glue will also be needed.

Knitted cover

With white yarn, cast on 40sts and follow the chart, see (Fig 2), as far as row 13.

Row 14: p11, turn and work on these sts separately, keeping the colour-pattern according to the chart as the shaping progresses.

Row 15: k2tog, k9.

Row 16: p10.

Row 17: k2tog, k8.

Row 18: p9.

Row 19: k2tog, k7.

Row 20: p6, p2tog in white.

Row 21: k2tog in green, k5.

Row 22: p4, p2tog.

Row 23: sl 1, k2 tog, psso, k2.

Row 24: sl 1, p2tog, psso.

Now work the RH side.

Row 14: (WS facing) join in the white yarn and k18, this is the drain-pipe ridge, p11 in white.

Row 15: Work on the first 11sts only, keeping the colour-pattern according to the chart as the shaping progresses, join in the green yarn, k9, k2tog.

Row 16: p10.

Row 17: k8, k2tog in white.

Row 18: p9.

Row 19: k7, k2tog.

Row 20: p2tog, p6.

Row 21: k5, k2tog.

Row 22: p2tog, p4.

Row 23: k2, sl 1, k2tog, psso.

Row 24: sl 1, p2tog, psso.

Now work on the centre 18sts, joining in the yarns again and beg on row 15, keeping the colour-pattern according to the chart. Row 24 is the last complete row worked in white only. Cast off. Darn ends in, etc.

Making up

For the card foundation, score lightly along the dotted lines, fold the sides backwards and secure with glue. From the WS sew up the two angled edges of the knitting and glue this shape firmly on to the card foundation. Match the edges on all sides and adjust the corners accurately. The edges at the back of the greenhouse can now be glued to the wall or house.

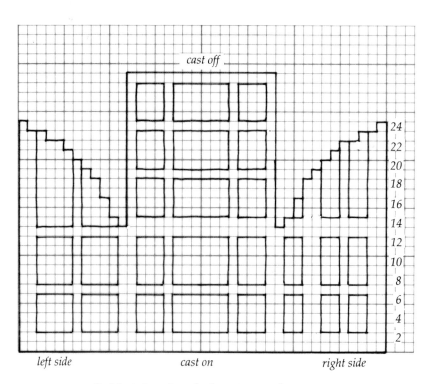

fig 2 **knitting chart for lean-to greenhouse**

LARGE COLD FRAME

Friary gardens

An essential part of the vegetable garden, the cold frame protects delicate plants and helps to harden off those at an in-between stage from greenhouse to the outside world. This one is made in a combination of stocking stitch and garter stitch over a card base.

Empty, it would make a delightful gift for a gardener friend: imagine the conversation, "Where did you put your ear-rings dear? What? In the cold frame?".

Measurements

As shown on the diagrams, see Figs 1a and 1b.

Materials

For the card foundation, stiff card measuring 32 × 28cm (12½ × 11in) from which to cut the two main pieces. Glue and parcel tape.
For the knitted cover, approximately 50gm (2oz) of off-white DK yarn and 25gm (1oz) of oddments of browns and greens. Silver metallic yarn is useful for the glass panels, but not essential. Size 3¾mm needles.

Card foundation

From the piece of stiff card, cut out the shape shown in the diagram for the base, see Fig 1a, scoring along the dotted lines. Fold these pieces inwards and bind the sections firmly in place with strong parcel tape. Cut out the lid, see Fig 1b, and leave aside for the moment.

Above: There is plenty of room in the large cold frame to nurture your cabbages and cauliflowers.

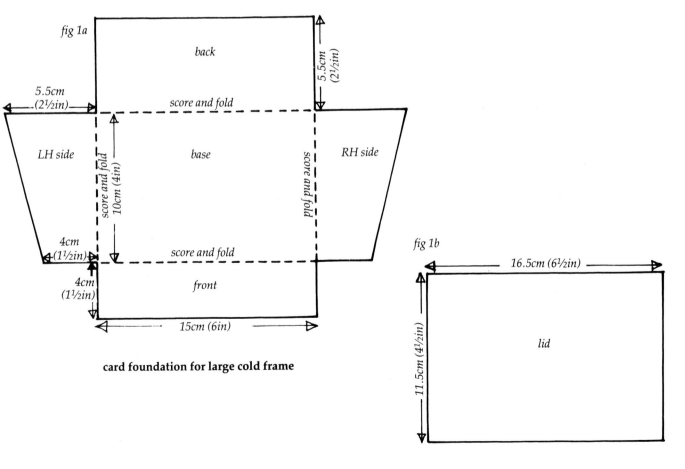

fig 1a

back

5.5cm (2½in)

5.5cm (2½in)

score and fold

LH side

score and fold

10cm (4in)

base

score and fold

RH side

4cm (1½in)

score and fold

4cm (1½in)

front

15cm (6in)

card foundation for large cold frame

fig 1b

16.5cm (6½in)

11.5cm (4½in)

lid

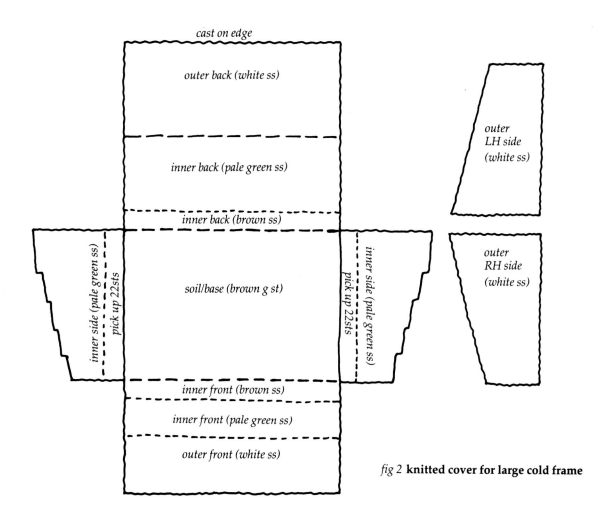

fig 2 **knitted cover for large cold frame**

Knitted cover for the large cold frame

Begin at the outer back as shown in the diagram, see Fig 2. Using off-white yarn, cast on 36sts and work in ss for 19 rows.

Row 20: knit, (rev ss), for the ridge across the top of the back section, then break off the yarn.

Row 21: join in pale green and work 10 rows in ss, weaving in the loose ends along the back of the first row.

Row 31: cut the green yarn and join in the brown. Work 5 more rows of ss.

Row 36: change to g st for the soil base, noting that the knitting will expand sideways, so the sts must be decreased accordingly to keep the sides straight. Try decreasing 3sts evenly along the row to 33sts and see how this looks. I found this worked quite perfectly. (Remember that the sts will have to be readjusted when you change back to ss).

Now work in brown g st for 10cm (4in), approximately 41 rows.

Next row: (RS facing) increase back to 36sts and work 4 rows of ss. Cut brown and join in pale green.

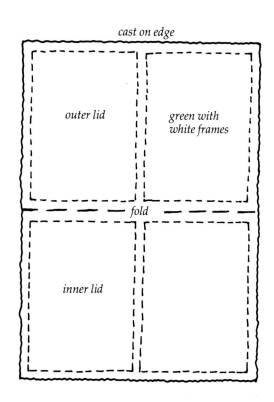

Work 4 rows of ss. Cut green yarn and join in white. Knit one row.

Next row: (WS) knit.

Continue in ss for 12 more rows to the lower edge of the front section, then cast off.

Inner side sections

These are made by picking up sts from the g st base instead of casting on and sewing up. However, the latter method may be used if you prefer.

Make the RH side piece first: with RS facing and using brown yarn, pick up 22sts from the RH side of the g st base, (not the ss parts), and work 3 rows in ss beg with a p row.

Change to pale green and continue in ss for 4 more rows.

Slope the top edge as follows:–

Row 8: (RS) cast off 4sts and k to end.

Row 9: p.

Repeat these 2 rows 3 more times, then cast off the last 6sts.

Make the LH side piece: with the RS facing and using brown yarn, pick up 22 sts from the LH side of the g st base and work 3 rows in ss beg with a p row.

Change to pale green and continue in ss for 5 more rows.

Slope the top edge as follows:–

Row 9: (WS) cast off 4sts p-wise and p to end.

Row 10: k.

Repeat these 2 rows 3 more times then cast off the last 6sts p-wise.

With RS tog, fold up the 4 corners and sew them up matching the brown and green sections. The inside lining is now complete.

Outer side sections

Work the 2 outer side sections as follows:– using white yarn, make the RH side first. Cast on 22sts and work 10 rows in ss.

Row 11: k18, turn, leaving the last 4sts on the LH needle and p back to the end of the row.

Row 13: k14, turn and p back.

Row 15: k10, turn and p back.

Row 17: k6, turn and p back.

Row 19: knit across all 22sts.

Cast off p-wise.

Make the LH side as follows:– cast on 22sts and work 9 rows in ss.

Row 10: p18, turn and k back.

Row 12: p 14, turn and k back.

Row 14: p10, turn and k back.

Row 16: p6, turn and k back.

Row 18: p across all 22sts.

Cast off.

With RS tog, pin and sew the 2 sloping edges of the inner and outer side sections. Now sew the back and side sections together, then the front and side sections, taking care to align the corners precisely. This will probably look too loose to fit the box but you will find that, as you glue each section, the knitting will shrink into place on the card.

Glue the soil (g st) base first: remember that all ss areas are side pieces. Continue to glue each section one by one, working from the inside to the outside and pulling each piece on to the card foundation. Nip the top edges to ensure a sharp outline.

Lid of the large cold frame

This is knitted from the back edge towards the front and then continues in one piece round to the other side to make a tube which is joined down the two side edges when the card is inside. As both sides will be more or less the same, you can choose which one is the best after you have made the complete lid, and then put it on top.

You can also choose whether to make this a loose slide-on-off lid, or whether to attach it along the back edge to make it lift up, as for the one illustrated. To keep the lid open on warm days, it could be propped up with a piece of wood!

Using white yarn, cast on 36sts and work 2 rows in ss. Now measure roughly 2m (2yd) of yarn from the needle and cut off. Cut 2 more lengths of white yarn and keep this ready to join in on the 3rd row. These are for the white lines running down each side and centre of the piece, avoiding the need to carry the white yarn across the row. The green yarn is used from the ball, so no weaving-in is necessary except the loose ends on the first row. However, remember to bring the new yarns from *underneath* the previous ones to twist them together, otherwise gaps will appear. If a length of yarn runs out, tie on a new one and weave the end in at the back.

Row 3: work in patt and k2 white, 15 green, 2 white, 15 green, 2 white.

Working in ss, rep this patt until 28 patt rows have been worked.

Next 2 rows: work in white yarn only, leaving the other strands of yarn hanging from the back to be picked up later. (These strands should be twisted with the knitting yarn, as before, as it passes along, to carry them upwards over the next 5 rows).

Next 2 rows: p in white only.

Next row: knit.

Next row: purl.

Now pick up the loose strands and work 28 more patt rows.

Next row: (RS) knit in white only, weaving in all other strands on the back.

Next row: purl.

Cast off.

With RS facing, sew up cast on and cast off edges to make a tube. Sew one side edge to make a pocket and turn to RS. Insert card into pocket and sew up other side edge. If the lid is to be hinged to lower section, sew the two cast on/off edges together neatly across the back from both outside and inside.

SMALL COLD FRAME
Cottage gardens

The knitted cover for this tiny version is made in one long rectangle, with two separate side sections. The main piece begins on the inside of the front edge and continues on to the outside front towards the base, back and lid, then the inside lid, inside back and finishes on the inside base, i.e the soil. It should fit the card quite closely, so if you discover that your knitting extends beyond the card shape, either make another card foundation or begin again on finer needles and/or finer yarn.

To prevent the edges of the stocking stitch rolling inwards, begin every row with a knit stitch. All outer sections are marked with a row of rev ss.

Materials

A small piece of stiff card for the foundation to the measurements on the diagram, see Fig 1. Sticky-tape can be used for binding the card shape.
For the knitted cover, oddments of DK white or wood colour, greens and browns and size 3¼mm needles.

Knitted cover for the small cold frame

Using white yarn, cast on 12sts and begin at the inside front edge as follows:–
Rows 1, 3, 4, 5 and 8: knit.
Rows 2, 6, 7 and 9: purl.
Cut off the white yarn.
For the outside base, change to brown yarn and beg with a p row, work 8 rows of ss. Cut off brown yarn.

Row 18: join in white yarn, and p one row to begin the back section.
Rows 19 and 20: purl.
Continue in ss for 8 more rows, beg with a knit row.
Row 29: purl.
Begin the lid section and join in the green yarn.
Row 30: p2 white, 4 green, 1 white, 4 green, 2 white.
Continue in this patt for 6 more rows.
Row 37: knit one complete white row and weave the green yarn in along the back to the other end of the row ready to pick up again on row 40.
Row 38: knit.
Row 39: purl.
Row 40: (inside lid) beg with a p row, repeat the colour patt of row 30 and work 4 more rows.
Cut the green yarn.
Row 45: knit one white row, weaving green end in on back.
Continue in ss for 9 rows to make the inside back section, beg with a p row. Cut white yarn and weave the end in on the next row.
Row 55: change to brown yarn for the inside base and work in g st for 10 rows, but decreasing one st in the centre of the first row to make 11sts.
Cast off and trim or darn in loose ends.

Side sections

Before you begin the two side sections, attach the main piece of knitting to the card frame as follows:–
beginning with the cast on edge on the inside of the front section, glue the card and press the knitting in place, matching all edges exactly. Do this section by section all round the outside of the frame, then the inside, finishing off with the soil in the cold frame. Push the corners well in and bend the card frame into shape as you glue each section. Now make the sides as follows, (no inside sections for these).
For the RH side, ** using white yarn, cast on 8sts and work 4 rows of ss **.
Row 5: k6, k2tog.
Row 6: sl 1, p1, psso, p5.
Row 7: k4, k2tog.
Row 8: cast off 2sts, p to end.

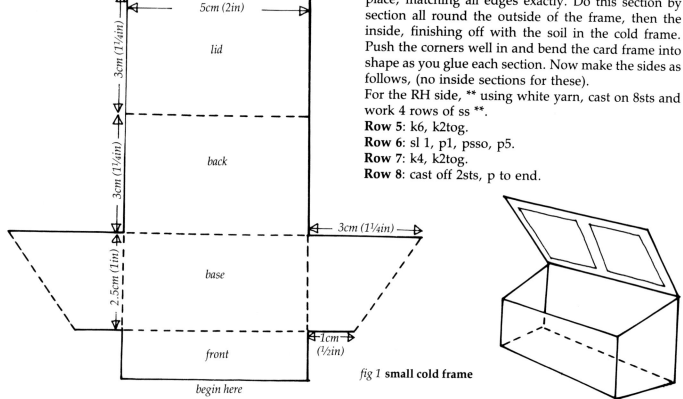

fig 1 **small cold frame**

Row 9: cast off last 3 sts.
For the LH side, work as RH side from ** to **.
Row 5: k2tog, k6.
Row 6: p5, sl 1, p1, psso.
Row 7: k2tog, k4.
Row 8: p1, (p2tog) twice.
Row 9: cast off last 3 sts.
Sew the lower edges of these pieces to the side bases of the cold frame then continue up the adjoining edges sewing the front, sides and back together. Stitch along the sides of the lid to close the two edges together. The tiny cucumber plant can be found on page 89.

LARGE CLOCHE
Friary gardens

If there is insufficient room in your garden for a cold frame, make a cloche to protect the plants.

Measurements
12.5 × 5cm (5 × 2in).

Materials
Small amounts of green 3ply yarn and metallic/glitter used together and dark green DK yarns. Size 4mm needles.
For the card foundation, an oblong piece of stiff card measuring 12.5 × 7.5cm (5 × 3½in), scored and folded down the centre to form a long V-shape.

Knitted cover
Cast on 20sts and work in ss for 17 rows, using green + metallic.
Row 18: leave green yarn hanging and join in dark yarn, purl one row.
Row 19: purl.
Cut dark yarn and pick up green/metallic.
Continue as before for 17 more rows. Cast off.

Darn ends in and glue the knitted piece on to the card with the dark stripe running across from one side to the other.
Make the end pieces as follows:– with dark green yarn, cast on 10sts and knit 2 rows.
Row 3: k2tog, k6, k2tog.
Rows 4, 5 and 6: k8.
Row 7: k2tog, k4, k2tog.
Rows 8, 9 and 10: k6.
Row 11: k2tog, k2, k2tog.
Rows 12, 13 and 14: k4.
Row 15: k2tog twice then cast off.

ROW OF CLOCHES
Cottages gardens

This is based on a strip of card measuring 3cm (1¼in) wide, with a line scored along the centre to form a V-shape. The length of it will be determined by the width of the plot for which it is needed.

The effect of sparkling glass is achieved by knitting sparkling metallic threads with a 3 or 4 ply coloured yarn in various combinations. The ones used here were two pale green 3plys, one blue and one silver Twilley's Gold-fingering, with a deep green to mark the divisions. Only very small oddments of yarn are needed and a pair of size 3¼mm needles.

Knitted cover
Cast on 8sts and work 10 rows of ss. Do not break the yarn but join in deep green and work 2 rows, then pick up the first yarn, cut the deep green and weave the ends in as you work the next cloche.
When your piece is long enough, glue the knitting to the card and fold it along its length. End pieces are not necessary, but the cloche may be glued or sewn on to the garden if required.

Small cold frame and row of cloches.

Tubs and containers

RAIN BARREL
Friary gardens

There is nothing as refreshing as rain for the garden and you can use this barrel for filling the watering can.

Measurements
9cm (3½in) in height, see illustration on page 72.

Materials
Two discs of card measuring 5.5cm (2¼in) and 5cm (2in) diameter, padding and glue.
For the knitted cover, an oddment of brown DK yarn, a very little black and size 4mm needles.

Knitted cover
Using brown yarn, cast on 32sts.
Rows 1 and 2: knit.
Row 3: purl.
Row 4: join in black yarn and knit.
Row 5: p. Cut black yarn.
Row 6: (k7, inc) 4 times, (36sts).
Row 7 and alt rows: purl.
Row 8: (inc, k8) 4 times, (40sts).
Row 10: (k7, inc) 5 times, (45sts).
Row 12: (inc, k8) 5 times, (50sts).
Row 14: k.
Row 16: (k2tog, k8) 5 times, (45sts).
Row 18: (k7, k2tog) 5 times, (40sts).
Row 20: (k2tog, k8) 4 times, (36sts).
Row 22: (k7, k2tog) 4 times, (32sts).
Row 23: join in black and purl.
Row 24: knit. Cut black.
Row 25: p.
Rows 26 and 27: k, then cast off.

Making up
Sew the 2 side edges together. The smaller disc of card is for the base, (i.e the cast off edge) and the larger one is for the water. Make the latter in silver-coloured card or foil.
Glue the base card in position and fill the barrel with padding, making an even curve and not too fat. Place the water disc on top of this and glue all round the inner rim, pulling the knitting over the edge of the card.

SMALL RAIN BARREL
Cottage gardens

This is a small-scale version especially for the villagers on Cottage Row.

Measurements
3.5cm (1½in) high.

Materials
Two discs of stiff card, one of them 3cm (1¼in) diameter and the other slightly larger. The smaller one is for the base.
Oddments of brown DK yarn, padding and glue. Size 3¼mm needles.

Knitted cover
Cast on 20sts and knit 2 rows.
Rows 3, 5, 7, 9, 11, 13 and 14: purl.
Row 4: (inc, k4) 4 times, (24sts).
Row 6: knit.
Row 8: (inc, k3) 6 times, (30sts).
Row 10: (k2tog, k3) 6 times, (24sts).
Row 12: (k2tog, k3) 4 times, k2tog, k2.
After row 14, cast off knit-wise. This edge is the bottom of the barrel.

Making up
Sew up the two side edges and push the smaller piece of card down to the bottom. Glue it in place just inside the rim. Insert padding to form a slightly rounded shape and glue the second piece of card on top of this. Push it down about 1cm (½in) from the top.

LARGE WOODEN TUB WITH SHRUBS
Friary gardens

This is shown in the friary garden and is illustrated on page 48.

Measurements
6 × 4cm (2½ × 1½in).

Materials
Oddments of brown and black DK yarns and size 3¾mm needles.
Strip of card measuring 21 × 4cm (8¼ × 1½in), joined to make a tube. A base is optional. The circumference of the tube is approximately 20.5cm (8in).

Knitted cover
With brown yarn, cast on 46sts and work 6 rows in ss. Change to black yarn, (do not cut brown), and k2 rows.

Rows 9 to 12: cut black yarn, pick up brown and work 4 rows in ss.
Rows 13 and 14: p.
Row 15: k.
Cast off.

Making up

Turn to WS and sew side edges tog. Turn to RS and slip this over the tube. Glue the inside rim of the wooden tub and fold the top rows of ss inside, with the rev ss ridge along the top edge of the tub, see Figs 2a and 2b.
Turn up the knitting to expose the card, glue the sides and fold the knitting back on to this, arranging the edge of the knitting on to the bottom edge.
Pack 2 or 3 pom-pons into the top and glue these in place.

FREE-STANDING TUB

This is shown with a tree on the opposite page.

Measurements

4 × 4cm (1½ × 1½in).

Materials

An oddment of stone-coloured DK yarn and some padding and card. Size 3¾mm needles.

Knitted cover

Casts on 24sts and knit 3 rows.
Row 4: (k4, p1) 4 times, k4.
Row 5: (p4, k1) 4 times, p4.
Rep rows 4 and 5 three more times, (i.e 8 rows of patt).
Next row: p.
Next row: k.
Rep the last 2 rows twice more then cast off.

Making up

For diagram, see Fig 1.

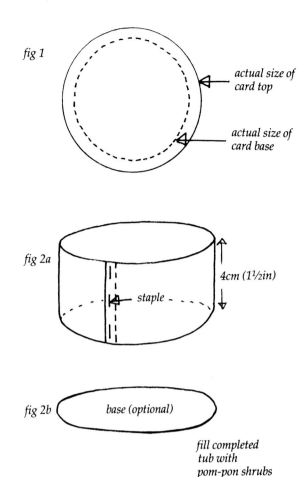

fig 1

actual size of card top

actual size of card base

fig 2a

staple

4cm (1½in)

fig 2b base (optional)

fill completed tub with pom-pon shrubs

free-standing tub and large wooden tub

STONE PLANT CONTAINER
Cottage gardens

Use the same instructions as for the tiny bee-skeps on page 76, but turn the shape upside-down and flatten the base instead of pointing it. Use stone-coloured yarn and change the stitch-pattern if you wish.

Tools of the trade

Whilst it is relatively easy to knit soft 'growing' things, or even round, three-dimensional and straight-sided things too, it is more difficult, and somewhat unconvincing, to knit spade handles and wheelbarrows. So, for tools, (which are essential in any garden, real or knitted), I have tried to compromise by using wood and, in one case only, a 'spade' of knitting for Brother Andrew who tells me that the worms prefer it!

The other tools, such as the fork, hoe, rake and dibber, are made from very thin lengths of wood, (bought from the DIY merchant), and tiny pieces of card, shaped and shaded in with felt-tipped pens and coloured pencils. All that is needed is the wood, card, a very sharp craft knife plus a steady hand, glue and colouring pens or pencils. Measure the length of the handles against your figures before you cut, and go from there; you will soon be able to tell how long they should be.

BROTHER ANDREW'S SPADE
Friary gardens

To make a replica of this spade, just cut a piece of card about 2.5cm (1in) square with the corners snipped off. Use oddments of grey and brown DK yarns and size 3¼mm needles. The shaft of the spade is wood.
Cast on 4sts and work in ss for 4 rows.
Row 5: inc in first and 4th sts to make 6sts.
Row 6 and 8: p.
Row 7: k.
Row 9: change to brown yarn and work in ss for 4 rows.

Row 13: p.
Row 14: k.
These 2 rows are the folding edge.
Rows 15 to 18: work in ss.
Cut brown and join in grey.
Rows 19 and 20: ss. Cast off.
Fold the piece across the 2 rows of rev ss with the WS tog, enclose the card square and sew up the side edges from the RS. Leave the top open with the 4sts at the upper end.
Place a dab of glue on the end of the wooden handle, (about 2.5cm (1in) along), and place this end into the pocket, pressing the knitting and card on to it until it is firmly stuck.
Sew up the top, wrapping the 4 cast on sts round the handle, (shaft), of the spade and pulling them together at the back.

SACK OF COMPOST
Friary gardens

You will need a small amount of off-white, brown or grey DK yarn and size 3¼mm needles.
Cast on 26sts and work in ss for 26 rows.
Fold this piece across the centre with the RS tog and sew up the side and the base. Turn to the RS, pad gently and run a gathering thread across each corner, drawing these up slightly to make points. Lettering is best written on gently with a felt-tipped pen.

WATERING CAN
Friary gardens

This is an essential piece of garden equipment and is used in the cottage gardens.

Measurements
6cm (2¼in) high.

Materials
Card tube from a roll of cooking foil, 3cm (1¼in) diameter × 4cm (1½in) long. Small disc of card for the base, glue.
Oddment of grey DK yarn and size 3¼mm needles.

Card foundation
Draw round the tube on to a piece of card, cut out this disc and glue it to the base of the tube.

Knitted cover
Cast on 28sts and work 12 rows in ss.
Row 13: cast off 7sts p-wise, p to the last 7sts, cast off 7sts and cut the yarn.
Row 14: join the yarn to the centre 14sts and purl, weaving in the end along the back, (WS).
Row 15: k2tog, k10, k2tog.
Row 16: p.
Row 17: k2tog, k8, k2tog.
Row 18: (p2tog) 5 times.

Cast off and darn the end in to make a smooth curve on this edge. Fold in half, RS tog, and sew side edges. Turn to RS and glue the piece on to the card tube.

For the spout, cast on 5sts and work 10 rows in ss

Row 11: (inc, k1) twice, inc in last st.

Cast off.

From the RS and the cast on edge, sew the piece down towards the wider end, leaving this open for about the last 3 rows. Darn in all ends.

Spread the wide end out to form a flat, semi-circular shape and glue this part on to the side of the can towards the bottom edge.

For the side handle, cast on 14sts and cast off again immediately. Sew this strip to the top and bottom edges of the can along the back seam.

For the top handle, make this in the same way as the side handle, or crochet a cord, and sew this to each side of the top edge of the can.

LARGE PLANT POTS
Friary gardens

The size can be varied by using more or less sts and rows.

Measurements
Basic large size measures 3cm (1¼in) high.

Materials
Tiny oddments of brick-coloured DK yarns, size 3¾mm needles and a tiny disc of card.

Knitted cover
Cast on 20sts and knit 2 rows.

Rows 3, 5, 7 and 9: purl.

Row 4: (k2tog, k8) twice.

Row 6: (k2tog, k7) twice.

Row 8: (k2tog, k6) twice.

Row 10: (k2tog, k5) twice.

Row 11: knit.

Row 12: k2tog 6 times.

Gather the last 6sts on to a wool needle and draw up to form the base of the pot. Sew up the side edges and darn ends in.

From stiff card, cut a tiny disc just big enough to fit inside the base and glue this in position to help the pot

to stand. A disc to represent topsoil may also be inserted at the top edge if needed.

For extra support when the pot has a plant inside, another larger piece of card may be glued to the outside base underneath the pot.

TINY PLANT POT
Cottage gardens

This is just large enough to go on the end of a little finger! Use the same yarn and needles as above.

Cast on 8sts and work 3 rows in ss.

Row 4: (p2tog, p1) twice, p2tog.

Row 5: p5.

Gather the last 5sts on to a wool needle and complete as above.

Garden extras

BENCH
Cottage gardens

Gardening can be hard work and it's pleasant to take a breather and check on the progress you have made!

Measurements
As shown in the diagram, see Fig 1.

fig 1 **card base for garden bench**

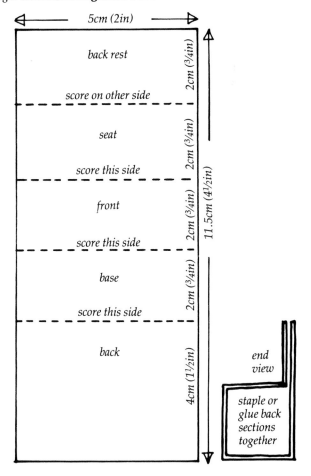

Pick a sunny spot in your garden for the bench.

Materials

A rectangle of stiff card and some glue.
For the knitted cover, oddments of brown, or white, and green DK yarns. Size 3¼mm needles.

Card foundation

To make the card foundation, cut the card as shown in the diagram, mark in the dotted lines and then score as shown, taking care to do this from the sides indicated. Fold this piece and glue, or staple in position.

Knitted cover

Using white cast on 24sts and knit one row.
Row 2: join in green, p2 white, 4 green, 2 white, 8 green, 2 white, 4 green, 2 white.
Row 3: k2 white, 4 green, 2 white, 8 green, 2 white, 4 green, 2 white.
Repeat these 2 rows once more.
Row 6: p in white only but do not cut green yarn.
Row 7: cast off 5sts p-wise, p to end of row.
Row 8: cast off 5sts k-wise, pick up green and strand loosely to next st and purl (1 white, 1 green) 3 times, 2 white, (1 green, 1 white) 3 times.
Keep this colour patt for 4 more rows in ss ending on a p row.
Row 13: leave green hanging and k in white only to end.
Row 14: knit.
Now continue in patt as before for 4 rows.
Rows 19 and 20: knit in white only.
For a wall-bench where the back will not be seen, cast off at this stage. If the bench is to be free-standing, continue in pattern for 10 more rows, then cast off. This extra piece will then cover the back.

Making up

Fold the 2 side pieces along the top edge of the seat as far as the ridge and sew in position. Now glue the card foundation and carefully position the knitted shape on to this, glueing the two side pieces to the edges of the card. The knitted back piece will extend slightly beyond the card at the top.
If an extra back has been made, the back and side sections should be sewn together before glueing.

FOUNTAIN
Friary gardens

This is made in three sections, the stand with a bowl at the top, the water for the bowl, and the pool at the base. In fact, the stand alone may be used as a bird-table and the pool as just a pool!

Measurements

Diameter of base roughly 11.5cm (4½in) and it stands roughly 6cm (2½in) high.

Materials

For the construction, 2 discs of card for the base which should be measured after the knitting has been done, though these are optional. Small amounts of padding for the stand.
For the knitted cover, roughly 20gm (¾oz) stone-coloured DK yarn and small amounts of Twilley's Goldfingering in silver and pale blue. Size 3¼ and 4mm needles.

Knitted stand and bowl

Using 3¼mm needles, and stone yarn, cast on 40sts for the edge of the bowl.
Rows 1, 3 and 4: knit.
Row 2: purl.
Row 5: k1, (y fwd, k2tog) 19 times, k1.
Rows 6 and 7: purl.

For the next 7 rows, work in double rib.

Row 15: (k2, p2tog) 10 times, (30sts).

Row 16: (k1, p2) 10 times.

Row 17: mark this row with a short length of coloured yarn, (k2tog, p1) 10 times, (20sts).

Row 18: (k1, p1) 10 times.

For the next 4 rows, work in single rib.

Row 23: inc into every st to make 40sts.

Rows 24, 25 and 26: knit.

Cast off loosely. The cast off edge is the base of the stand.

Make up the stand

Before you knit the water, make up the stand by beginning at the top and sewing the 2 edges tog as far as the marker on row 17. Leave the thread hanging. Begin sewing again at the base and close the edges towards the marker, take one or two back sts to secure the last st, then take a running st half-way round the stem at row 17. With the hanging thread, do the same in the other direction. When the two threads meet at the opposite side, pull the fabric up tightly to close the bowl and then secure both threads.

Pad the lower section slightly to fill out the base of the stand and glue a small disc of card inside the edge to keep the padding flat.

Make the water

Using double metallic yarn and size 4mm needles, cast on 40sts and knit 6 rows.

Row 7: (k2tog) 20 times and gather these sts on to a wool needle.

Draw up tightly and sew up the two edges to form a circle. Sew this piece inside the bowl, pushing it down slightly towards the centre. Tie a few wisps of glitter and white yarns together into a bundle and push the knot down into the centre hole to represent water jets.

LARGE BEE-SKEPS
Friary gardens

The friars have always relied on the industrious bees for sweetening in their food and skeps play an important role in the garden.

Measurements

6.5 ×5cm (2½ × 2in). On the stand, 10cm (4in) high.

Materials

About 10gm (½oz) of straw-coloured DK yarn for each one and size 4mm needles.

Shaped piece of foam or padding and a small piece of card, see the diagram Fig 1 for the stand and the doorway. Glue.

Stand construction

Make this as shown in the diagram and use coloured pencils or paints to colour the legs and spaces. Do not cut the legs out of the card. Glue a slightly larger oblong piece of card on top of the stand as shown in the lower diagram.

Knitted cover

Cast on 30sts and knit 4 rows.
Rows 5, 6, 8, 9, 12, 15, 16, 18, 19 and 22: purl.
Rows 7, 10, 11, 13, 14, 17 and 20: knit.
Row 21: (k2tog, k3) 6 times, (24sts).
Row 23: (k2tog, k2) 6 times, (18sts).
Row 24: knit.
Gather the last sts on to a wool needle and draw up to form the domed top of the skep. Sew up the side edges matching the ridges.
Use a piece of shaped foam or pad to form a rounded shape as shown. Glue this shape to the top of the stand and cut a tiny doorway for the bees. Glue this in place at the bottom, then embroider tiny bees in clusters round the doorway.

TINY BEE-SKEPS
Cottage gardens

These stand about 3cm (1¼in) high along the high garden wall. Very small amounts of pale straw-coloured DK yarn is needed, and some brown to embroider the doorway. Use size 3¼mm needles.

Knitted cover

Cast on 14sts and work in ss for 5 rows.
Row 6: (inc, k6) twice.
Knit 8 rows.
Row 15: (k2tog) 8 times.
Row 16: k8.
Row 17: (k2tog) 4 times.
Thread the 4sts on to a wool needle, gather up tightly and secure the end. Sew up the sides from the WS to form a cone shape. Turn to the RS then push the ss section down into the cone to form a lining. Ease the knitting into shape at the top to form a rounded point and embroider 3 or 4 brown satin sts at the base for the doorway. Tiny brown beads may be sewn on to the hive to represent bees.
Note: these instructions will also work perfectly for the small stone plant container, turned upside-down and with the base flattened a little.

fig 1 **large bee-skep**

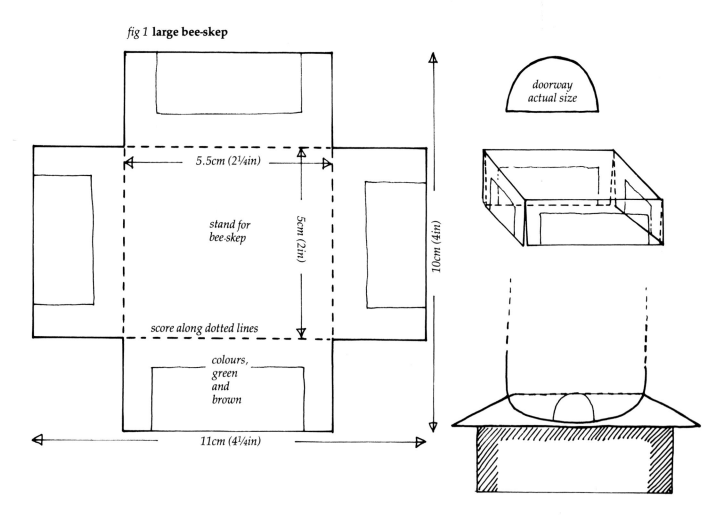

Planting your garden

Whether you wish to stock your garden with flowers,
fruit, trees or vegetables, a browse through
this chapter is recommended. It will give you
ideas you may not have considered and help you to make
a choice, as well as suggestions for filling
odd spaces. The plants are given in a range of sizes
suitable for the various projects and are
extremely simple to make.

Trees, bushes and hedges

SMALL CONIFER
House pillow

This little tree has many uses as a space filler in the garden and is seen in tubs outside the house pillow. It is easy to make, being entirely in garter stitch. A slightly larger version can be made using double yarns and thicker needles. A range of dark greens suggests different varieties, but note that some conifers are relatively light and some tend towards blue and yellow.

Materials
Green DK yarn and size 3¼mm needles. Padding.

Knitted cover
Cast on 25sts and knit 4 rows.
Row 5: k2tog, k to last 2sts, k2tog.
Row 6 and alt rows: knit.
Row 7: k11, k2tog, k10.
Rows 9, 13, 17, 21, 25: as row 5.
Row 11: k9, k2tog, k9.
Row 15: k8, k2tog, k7.
Row 19: k6, k2tog, k6.
Row 23: k5, k2tog, k4.
Row 27: k3, k2tog, k3.
Row 29: k2tog, k3, k2tog.
Row 31: k2, k2tog, k1. Cast off.

Making up
Fold in half lengthways and sew up the side edges, see Fig 1. Leave the base open, pad the cavity, gather the lower edges and sew up to form the base. A disc of card may be glued to the base to make standing easier.

SIMPLE TUBE POM-PON TREES
Cottage gardens

The simplest of all trees are these tube-based versions suitable for children to make. Consisting of three main elements, the tube trunk, the card disc base and the pom-pon top, they can be as large or as small as you wish, left plain or decorated with fruit. The trunks can also be made even more textural with lengths of French knitting wound round.

Materials
Cardboard tubes, (toilet-roll middles are useful for this), a disc of card for the base, (draw round a tea-cup).
Any green and brown DK, or thicker yarns, plain or textured. Size 4mm needles and glue.

Pom-pon trees
There are various methods of making the trees, which are basically an oblong of garter stitch sewn into a tube to cover the trunk. Glue a huge pom-pon, or several,

on to the top of this. The bases can be made in various ways as follows:–

1. Cast on 50sts and work in single rib for about 6 rows. Sew up the 2 short sides to form a ring and glue this round the base, slightly angled against the tree.
2. Use tiny bundles of coloured yarns to look like foliage. Glue these directly on to the card base.
3. In the same coloured yarn as the trunk, cast on 50sts then change to stone-coloured yarn and knit 4 rows. Cast off. This ring is then sewn up as in No 1 to look like a stone enclosure.
4. For an autumn tree, cast on 50sts in chestnut brown and work in moss st for about 5 rows. Sew up and glue as before.

CONE-SHAPED TOPIARY TREE
Friary gardens

A very simple way to make this type of tree is to wrap a cone with yarn, instead of knitting a cover. This is a speedy method and is how several of our garden trees were formed. I used thick, dark green chenille yarn which I had been hoarding for many years, knowing that someday it would be just the thing! Simply glue the edge of the yarn to the widest part of the cone and begin to wrap from the base upwards, laying the yarn close together as you go. Then dab on more glue at the top and press the yarn firmly in place. Any fluffy or highly textured yarn will do for this; you can even change yarns on the same tree.

This version is knitted in ss but, as has already been mentioned, both sides of this stitch can be used to create a different texture.

Measurements
Made on a machine-knitting cone, measuring 18 × 7cm (7 × 2¾in), see illustration opposite. The smaller measurement is the diameter.

Materials
Amounts of textured DK yarns in green. Size 3¾mm needles. Read the notes on colour given with the instructions for the small conifer.

Knitted cover
Use DK yarn and size 3¾mm needles and cast on 48sts.
Work 2 rows ss.
Row 3: (k2tog, k21) twice, k2tog.
Work 5 rows ss.
Row 9: k14, k2tog, k13, k2tog, k14.
Work 5 rows ss.
Row 15: k2tog, k39, k2tog.
Work 5 rows ss.
Row 21: k12, k2tog, k13, k2tog, k12.
Work 5 rows ss.

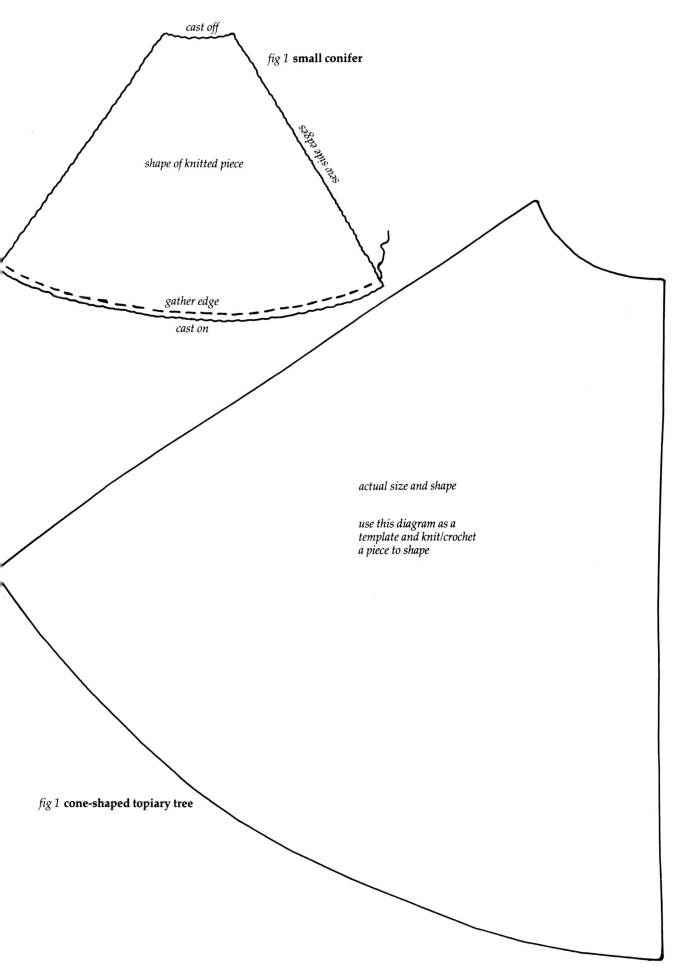

cast off

fig 1 **small conifer**

shape of knitted piece

sew side edges

gather edge

cast on

actual size and shape

use this diagram as a template and knit/crochet a piece to shape

fig 1 **cone-shaped topiary tree**

Row 27: k2tog, k17, k2tog, k16, k2tog, (36sts).
Work 3 rows ss.
Row 31: k11, k2tog, k10, k2tog, k11.
Work 3 rows ss.
Row 35: (k2tog, k14) twice, k2tog, (31sts).
Work 3 rows ss.
Row 39: (k6, k2tog) 3 times, k7.
Purl one row, and all following alt rows.
Row 41: (k2tog, k11) twice, k2tog.
Row 43: (k7, k2tog) twice, k7.
Row 45: (k4, k2tog) 3 times, k5.
Row 47: (k3, k2tog) 4 times.
Row 49: (k2tog) 8 times.
Purl one more row, cut yarn and thread through rem 8sts.

Making up

Gather up the top and sew down the sides from the WS, see Fig 1.
Note: if your knitted cover is too long, just turn up the extra inside the cone. If it is too short, either crochet a few rows on to the bottom edge, or knit on, or make a knitted strip to be sewn or glued on. This could also add a decorative touch to your tree!

THREE-DECKER TOPIARY BUSH
Cottage gardens

The foundation of this upright three-decker bush consists of a piece of wooden dowel around which three pieces of foam have been arranged, see illustration on page 40. The diagram shows the exact size of these units. The foam pieces are slid on to the dowel through a small hole cut into the centre of each:

it is quite easy to trim these foam pieces into shape with sharp scissors, but keep your index finger well out of the way!
Important note: always measure the girth of each piece with a tape measure and check the number of stitches on your needle. One or two more or less will make a difference. At the same time, remember that knitting stretches and the foam will squeeze inwards to give a neat tight fit.

Measurements

A piece of wooden dowelling measuring 13cm (5in) long, and three pieces of foam, measurements as shown in the diagram, see Fig 1.
For the cover, about 20gm (½oz) dark green DK yarn and size 4mm needles.

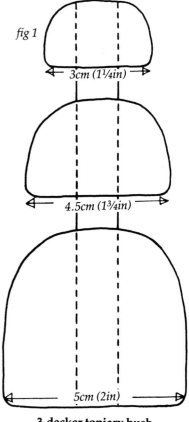

fig 1

3cm (1¼in)

4.5cm (1¾in)

5cm (2in)

3-decker topiary bush

Knitted cover

Enough knitting has been allowed for about 1cm (½in) to be turned under the base of the foam. The reverse side of the ss is the RS and the cover is made all-in-one piece in just 49 rows. However, if you want to make your tree shorter, just stop at the second dome. If your knitted cover does not fit the shape you have made, either trim the shape to fit or add synthetic padding underneath or at the sides.
Begin at the base and cast on 36sts. Work in ss for 14 rows.

Row 15: (k2tog, k2) 9 times, (27sts).
Row 16 and alt rows: purl.
Row 17: (k2tog, k1) 9 times, (18sts).
Row 19: (k2tog) 9 times.
Work 5 rows straight, then inc for the underside of the second dome as follows:–
Row 25: inc once into every st, (18sts).
Row 27: (inc, k1) 9 times, (27sts).
Row 29: (inc, k8) 3 times, (30sts).
Work 5 rows straight, then dec for the top:–
Row 35: (k2tog, k1) 10 times, (20sts).
Row 37: (k2tog) 10 times.
Work 5 rows straight, then inc for the underside of the third dome as follows:–
Row 43: (k1, inc one st into next 4sts) twice, (18sts).
Work 3 rows straight, then dec for the top as follows:–
Row 47: (k2tog) 9 times.
Row 49: (k2tog) 4 times, k1.
Gather these last sts on to a wool needle.

Making up

Fit the knitted piece over the foundation and draw the edges together. Stick pins through the knitting and into the foam to hold them in place. It is easier to sew accurately by working from both ends towards the middle from the RS using the flat seam. Pull the lower edge slightly over on to the underside. You may find it helpful to cut a piece of stiff card about 5–5.5cm (2–2¼in) in diameter and glue this on to the bottom for extra firmness. Alternatively, you could crochet a circle and sew this on instead. Gently manipulate the cover into place after sewing.

LONG YEW HEDGE
Friary gardens

The long box-shaped yew hedge acts as both a shelter and a border to the gardens within its boundaries, see illustration on page 48. Knit some in mid and dark green tones to represent beech, or privet, or yew. Though some of these are crocheted, only knitted instructions are given here.

Measurements

The hedge is based on a foam block measuring 29 × 7.5 × 6.5cm (11½ × 3 × 2½in).

Materials

For each hedge, a piece of foam to the above dimensions, though card may be used if preferred. Allow 50gm (2oz) of DK yarn for each hedge, but if you are making as many as eight, only seven 50gm (2oz) balls will be needed. Size 4mm needles.

Knitted cover

Cast on 60sts and work in double moss st for approximately 96 rows or until the piece measures 28cm (11in). Cast off and make the end pieces, allowing 2 for each hedge. Cast on 16sts and work in double moss st for 26 rows. Cast off.

Making up

Wrap the foam block in the knitting, pinning the cast on and cast off edges together along one edge of the block as shown in the diagram, see Fig 1. Sew these

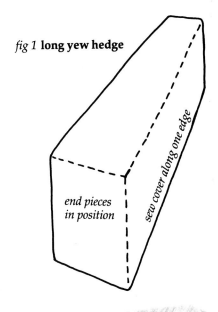

fig 1 **long yew hedge**

end pieces in position

sew cover along one edge

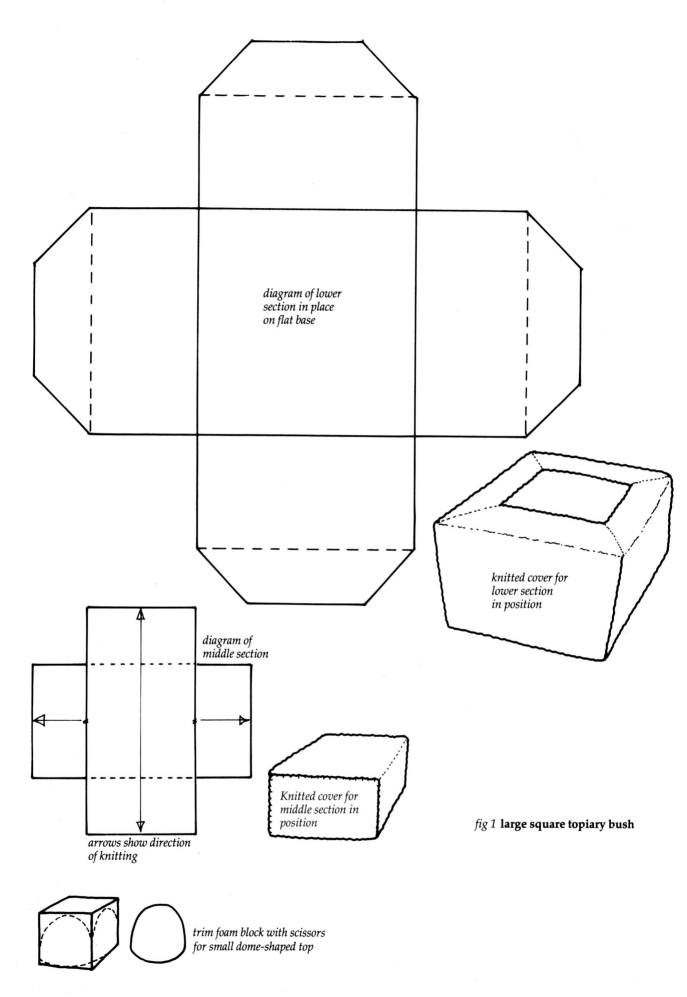

diagram of lower section in place on flat base

knitted cover for lower section in position

diagram of middle section

arrows show direction of knitting

Knitted cover for middle section in position

fig 1 **large square topiary bush**

trim foam block with scissors for small dome-shaped top

together from the RS then stretch the cover towards each end and pin the end pieces in position. Sew these on from the RS.

LARGE SQUARE TOPIARY BUSH
Friary gardens

This square-cut bush, in three sections, is useful as a corner-piece in a garden and, like the long hedge, can be made in any shade of green. Mottled and tweedy yarns are especially effective and when combined with double moss stitch, give an authentic leafy texture to the knitting, see illustration on page 48. As with the other bushes, this is based on pieces of shaped foam but card can be used if preferred.

Measurements
The bush stands approxiamtely 14cm (5½in) high and the base measures 15cm (6in) square.

Materials
For the foam foundation, cut the following for every bush: one piece 15 × 15 × 7.5cm (6 × 6 × 3in); one piece 7.5 × 7.5 × 4cm (3 × 3 × 1½in); one piece 4 × 4 × 2cm (1½ × 1½ × ¾in) but, if you prefer, this piece can be replaced by soft padding material.
For the knitted cover allow 50gm (2oz) DK in green. Size 3¾mm needles.

Knitted cover
Begin with the square base, see Fig 1. This piece fits on to the bottom of the bush but, as it will not be seen, any leftover bits of yarn can be used, so you may prefer to leave it until last. Another alternative is to make it first and then pick up stitches from the edges and knit the sides. However, the instructions are given for separate pieces.
For the lower section: cast on 36sts and work 44 rows in ss. Cast off.
Now make four separate side/top sections as follows:– cast on 32sts and work in double moss st for 26 rows. Begin the top shaping:–
Row 27: k2tog, patt to last 2 sts, k2tog.
Row 28: work in patt to end of row.
Repeat these last 2 rows once more, (28sts), and then row 27 twice more, i.e 2 decrease rows tog.
Repeat row 28. Repeat rows 27 and 28 twice more, (20sts). Cast off in patt.
Note: if you wish to cover the top completely for a small square box-bush, continue to decrease until no stitches rem.
For the centre section: make this in one piece with the two side pieces knitted on as shown in the diagram. Cast on 18sts and work in double moss st for 54 rows. Cast off in patt. To work the sides, fold this piece in half to find the centre of each long side. Measure 4cm (1½in) from the centre fold in both directions and mark with pins so that there is a 7.5cm (3in) section between

pins on each side. With the RS facing, pick up and knit 18sts between the markers and work 13 rows in double moss st on both sides. Cast off in patt.
The small dome-shaped top section: use a loose cast on and make 22sts. Work 12 rows in double moss st.
Row 13: (k2tog) 11 times.
Rows 14 and 15: single moss st.
Do not cast off but gather the last sts on to a wool needle.

Making up
Follow the diagram and sew the four lower sections to the base along the bottom edges, then sew up the sides as far as the shaping.
Now fit this piece over the foam block and pin the shaped pieces at the top in place by pushing pins into the knitting and through the foam. Sew up the top pieces from the RS to fit flat against the foam leaving a bare square in the centre. This is where the centre section fits.
Following the diagram, pin sides together and sew from the WS. Turn to RS and fit over the foam block, arranging the corners carefully. Place this piece on to the base of the hedge, and stitch all round from the RS securely.
For the top piece, sew the sides from the gathered top to the lower edge and run a gathering thread all round the lower edge. Draw this up gently and ease the lower edge of the knitting just underneath the foam block, (to hide the edge). Fit this piece on top of the centre piece and sew in place all round the edge.

LONG GREEN HEDGE
Cottage gardens

This very long hedge can be used to divide one cottage from another.

Measurements
53.5 × 4cm (21 × 1½in).

Materials
A strip of card to the above measurements will be needed, plus glue and synthetic padding.

For this small project, use up oddments of greens, browns and mixtures, bearing in mind that hedges turn brown and gold in winter and vary from very pale to deep green. Privet hedges may be yellow and many types are variegated. Instructions are given for DK yarns on size 4mm needles.

Knitted cover
Knit a strip measuring about 7.5cm (3in) wide, by 53.5cm (21in) long. This will require about 16sts. Fold this in half lengthways and sew up the two short ends. Enfold a piece of thick padding inside the knitting and pin the long edges together. Sew up from the RS and squeeze into shape.

Place a long line of glue along the centre of the card and glue the tube of knitting on to this to keep it upright. The two extending edges of the card base can be pushed underneath the gardens on each side of it. This helps to keep it secure.

ESPALIER FRUIT TREES
Cottage gardens

Fruit trees are often trained to grow in this decorative way, sometimes against a wall, as seen in the cottage gardens, sometimes on a wire or rail. When the branches are spread out in this way, they take up less room than normally. Various traditional arrangements are possible, some of them shown here, and these can be crocheted or embroidered directly on to the wall.

In either method, it is probably easier to do this before the wall is glued into place on the card foundation, but it *can* be done later if necessary. The crochet version is given below.

Crochet espalier tree
1. Begin with 20ch, see Fig 1. In the 3rd ch from the hook, work 5ch up the stem from the base. Now work 10ch for the first branch. Cut yarn.
2. Rejoin yarn (at No 2 on the diagram), with a slip st into the stem and make 10ch. Cut yarn.
3. Rejoin yarn (No 3) and work 3dc upwards into the stem. Then work 8ch. Cut yarn.
4. Rejoin yarn and work 8ch. Cut yarn.
5 and 6. Continue in the same way for the 2 top branches of 6ch each.

Leave a few cm (in) of yarn at the end of each branch for sewing on to the wall. Pin the shape on to the wall, then sew down each branch and stem with small back sts.

Note: the US equivalent of dc is single crochet.

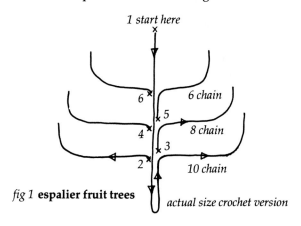

fig 1 **espalier fruit trees**   *actual size crochet version*

alternative espalier shapes

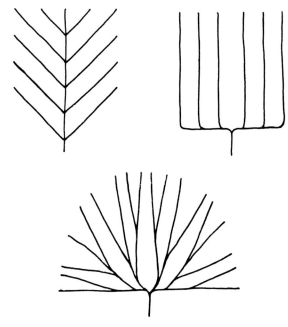

84

Fruit and vegetables

LARGE CABBAGES AND CAULIFLOWERS
Friary gardens and garden cushion

Two sizes of needles are used, 6mm and 4mm. The thicker ones are used for the cast on rows of the outer and inner leaves but not for the centres. This gives a loose and frilly edge. The finer ones are used for the tighter centres.

Each plant is made in three parts, inner and outer circles and inner dome. There is no casting off given in the instructions, as all the stitches are gathered on to the last thread and sewn with this.

Measurements
Diameter approximately 6cm (2¼in). The outer leaves roughly measure 6cm (2¼in) across but this can be varied by using different yarns and needle sizes. Tension is not important.

Materials
Use any combination of DK yarns plus any 3 or 4 plys. Metallic yarns are especially useful to suggest a moist shimmer on the leaves. Tiny oddments will do perfectly as hardly any two are exactly the same. The thickness of the yarn is not vitally important either, as long as the stitches do not become too gross in scale. The outer leaves are usually darker than the inner ones, so about three different tones of green will be needed, though four or five give an even greater variety and choice of permutations. The red and ornamental cabbages are very colourful, (look at seed packets and catalogues for ideas), and, for the centres of the cauliflowers, a creamy white yarn will be needed, textured if possible. A little padding will be needed for the centres.

Basic pattern
This can be varied and adapted in any way you choose. Leave long-ish ends at the cast on and finishing stages as these are used for sewing to the background. Glitter yarns should be darned in though, as these are difficult to sew with.

For the outer leaves: use size 6mm needles and a loose cast on to make 30sts. Knit one row.
Change to size 4mm needles and work in double rib for 4 rows.
Next row: (k2tog, p2tog) 15 times.
Work one row in single rib.
Cut the yarn and gather the last sts on to a wool needle. Pass the needle through the sts once more and tighten. Sew up the side edges to make a circle.
For the inner ring of leaves: use size 6mm needles, and loose cast on to make 20sts. Knit one row.
Change to size 4mm needles and work in double rib for 4 rows. Cut yarn and complete as outer leaves.
Thread the wool needle with the tail-ends and take

them down through the centre hole of the outer leaves.
Hold the two sections together firmly, exactly centred one inside the other, then stitch all round the hole allowing each stitch to go down through the centre and come up to one side of it each time. Fasten off and leave the tail on the outer leaves hanging free.
The centre dome: use size 4mm needles and cast on 10 sts. Work 4 rows in ss then gather sts on to a wool needle and sew up the side edges. *The reverse side is the RS.*
Place a tiny piece of padding in the centre, gather up and sew. Place this in the centre of the leaves and stab-stitch all round, (each stitch is made in two

Above: This row of sturdy cabbages will delight the keen gardener.

moves, one up and one down) and into the leaves beneath. Finish off securely. Pull the outer leaves upwards to enclose the firm centre and even out the stitches to frill them a little.

TINY CABBAGES
Cottage gardens

These are seen in the cottage garden, but can be used to fill odd gaps in your garden.

Materials
Oddments of mid to deep blue/green DK yarns and, for red cabbages, blue-red. Size 3¼mm needles.

Basic pattern
For the inner section: leave a tail of about 10cm (4in), cast on 10sts and knit one row.
Row 2: (k2tog) 5 times.
Leave a tail as before and gather the last sts on to a wool needle. Use the cast on tail to sew the sides to form a cup-shape and leave the yarn hanging from the bottom.
For the outer section: leave a tail as before, cast on 18sts and knit one row.
Row 2: (k2tog) 9 times.
Gather the sts on to a wool needle and complete as inner section. Thread the tails through the middle of the outer section then take these down into the garden plot about 1cm (½in) apart so that they can be tied together underneath. Trim the ends.

TINY CAULIFLOWERS
Cottage gardens

These are made in the same way as the tiny cabbages but make the inner section in a creamy-white yarn, with a little padding inside and invert it when fixing it to the outer section.

ONE-PIECE TINY CABBAGE OR LETTUCE
Cottage gardens

This is a very quick version of the tiny cabbage which also does very well for lettuce. Only about 3m (3½yd) of DK yarn is needed for each one. Use size 4mm or 3¼mm needles and leave long-ish ends when casting on and off.

Basic pattern
Cast on 24sts, (or 18 for a smaller size) using a loose cast on. Knit the first row and then, on alt rows, begin by casting off 6sts until no more are left.
With the narrow end innermost, coil this strip into a neat round shape and use the two tails to sew it in

position. Take both tails through to the underside of the garden plot, a little way apart, and tie them together.

LETTUCE
Friary gardens

This is a version of the large cabbage and is shown in the large cold frame.

Measurements
About 5cm (2in) across.

Materials
Oddments of pale green DK, 3 or 4 plys. Sizes 6mm, 4mm and 3mm needles and a little padding.

Basic pattern
For the outer leaf circle, use double yarn on 6mm needles and cast on 14sts loosely.
Rows 1 and 2: single rib.
Row 3: change to size 4mm needles and single rib.
Gather the sts on to a wool needle, draw up and sew up the side edges.
For the centre, use single yarn on size 3mm needles and cast on 10sts. Work in g st for 4 rows.
Gather as before, sew the side edges and pad inside. Sew this dome into the centre of the outer leaves.

TINY LETTUCE
Cottage gardens

Follow the same directions as for the tiny cabbages, but use a finer pale green yarn and finer needles.

CARROTS
Vegetable basket and garden cushion

These can be used to fill odd gaps in your garden.

Measurements
4cm (1½in) long.

Materials
Tiny oddments of orange and green DK yarns, size 3¼mm needles and padding.

Basic pattern
With orange yarn, cast on 8sts and work in ss for 6 rows.
Row 7: (k2tog, k1) twice, k2tog.
Row 8: p5.
Row 9: k1, k2tog, k2.
Row 10: p4.
Row 11: (k2tog) twice. Cast off.
Use the first tail to sew up the side edges, leaving the

Above: Fill your basket with all the succulent vegetables grown in your garden.

top open. Pad very lightly and squeeze into shape. Keep the top open.

Wrap green yarn round three fingers 4 or 5 times, cut this open and tie an over-hand knot in the middle to make a bundle. Fold this in half and push the knot down into the open end of the carrot. Gather the top edge with the orange yarn and tighten securely. Fasten off by taking the needle several times through the top edge from one side to the other. Fray the tops and trim ends.

CARROT TOPS IN SOIL
Friary gardens

Turnips and swedes can be made in the same way too, to look as though they are growing.

Materials

Tiny oddments of orange and green DK yarns and size 3¼mm needles.

Basic pattern

Cast on about 10sts with orange and knit one row. Gather these sts on to a wool needle, tying the yarn together with the other tail to pull the piece into a circle. Tie this very tightly.

Thread green yarn into a wool needle and make several loops into the top of the carrot, fastening off securely on the underside. Cut the loops and fray them with the points of the scissors. Glue or sew the carrot tops in rows on to the garden plot.

TINY CARROT BUNCHES
Cottage gardens

Use these to fill your vegetable patch.

Materials

Tiny oddments of orange DK yarn, dark green for the tops and size 3¼mm needles.

Basic pattern

Cast on 4sts with orange.

Rows 1 and 3: knit.
Row 2: purl.
Row 4: (k2tog) twice.
Row 5: k2tog and finish off.

Sew up the 2 edges to form a pointed carrot-shape and darn ends in. When you have made several of these, make a tiny bunch of dark green yarn, tie it in the centre and stitch it to the tops of the carrots to make a bunch.

CELERY
Vegetable basket and garden cushion

Crisp, crunchy celery is a must in any garden!

Measurements
7cm (2¾in) long.

Materials
Tiny oddments of creamy-white and two pale-green DK yarns. Size 3¼mm and 6mm needles and padding.

Basic pattern

With white yarn, cast on 10sts and work in single rib for 14 rows. Change to palest green and continue for 4 more rows. Change to deeper green and continue for 2 more rows. Change to 6mm needles and knit 2 rows. Cast off loosely.

Using the white yarn at the cast on edge, gather the lower edge, roll a small piece of padding inside the shape only as far as the first green row and sew up the two side edges as far as the 14th row.

Fasten off, then use the remaining green tail to sew downwards along the edge. Fasten off by taking the thread through the padding to the other side, keeping the top open.

LEEKS
Vegetable basket

You don't have to be Welsh to appreciate these!

Measurements
5cm (2in) long.

Materials
Oddments of creamy-white and three tones of green DK yarns, ranging from pale to deep green. Size 3¼mm needles.

Basic pattern

Using white yarn, cast on 5sts and work in ss for 6 rows. Change to palest green and work 4 rows. Change to mid-green and work 4 rows. Change to deep green and work 4 rows. Cast off.

Fold the piece in half lengthways and sew up from the RS, leaving the dark green top open. No padding needed.

ONION
Vegetable basket and garden cushion

These can be strung together and stored in the tool shed.

Measurements
Fractionally smaller than the swede, see opposite.

Materials
Gold/brown, beige and metallic gold DK yarns. Size 3¼mm needles and size 3.00mm crochet hook. Padding.

Basic pattern

Using combined gold/brown and metallic yarns, cast on 8sts, leaving a long-ish tail. Work 4 rows in ss. Change to beige and work 2 rows.

Row 7: (k2tog) 4 times.

Gather these 4sts on to a wool needle and leave open at this stage. Thread the cast on tail through a needle and gather the lower edge, at the same time placing a pad of stuffing into the space. Sew up the 2 side edges, (forming the end into a rounded shape), only as far as the 4th row. Tighten the neck by taking a running st all round the 4th row several times, leaving the 2 rows above this open. Fasten off.

Make the dried-up tops by crocheting 3 or 4 short chains of between 6 and 10ch each. Sew the ends of

Above: Close-up details of the vegetables decorating the garden cushion.

these down inside the open top of the onion, then tighten the top thread and fasten off.

Make a few loops at the base, keeping them about 7.5cm (3in) long so that they can be tied in an over-hand knot near the base of the onion. This prevents them being pulled out. Trim the ends irregularly and fray out.

SWEDE
Garden cushion

This is a delicious root vegetable, ideal for soups and casseroles.

Measurements
2cm (¾in) across.

Materials
Tiny oddments of tweedy-mauve and biscuit-coloured DK yarns, and green. Size 3¼mm needles and padding.

Basic pattern
With mauve yarn, cast on 12sts and work 6 rows in ss. Change to biscuit yarn.
Row 7: (k2tog) 6 times.
Row 8: p6.
Gather the last 6 sts on to a wool needle, take the needle through the sts once more and draw up tightly. Finish off. Run a gathering thread through the cast on edge, using the tail. This is the top. Pad inside the cavity and sew up the side edges. Make a feathery top as for the carrots.
The point at the base is made by using doubled biscuit yarn and embroidering tiny satin sts piled up on top of each other on one spot.

TINY CUCUMBER PLANT
Cottage gardens

This is for the small cold frame. Use oddments of various green DK yarns and size 3¼mm needles. Cast on 10sts and work one row single rib. Gather these sts on to a wool needle and draw up. This makes one leaf. Repeat this as many times as required and glue them to the base of the cold frame.
The fruit is made on 4sts. Work 8 rows ss, gather the end up on to a wool needle, curl the piece across and sew the side edges together. Glue or sew this in position.

ROW OF PEAS
Cottage gardens

Using 2 different DK green yarns together, (i.e double), and size 4½mm needles, cast on 5sts and work in moss st for the length needed to fit the garden plot. Cast off and fold in half lengthways. Sew the 2 long edges together and then sew or glue this on to the plot of soil.
Alternatively, for an even bumpier looking row, estimate the number of sts needed for the length of the row, (I used 17sts), then knit long rows of moss st, (about 6), instead of short ones.

RHUBARB
Cottage gardens

This grows profusely in the garden and makes delicious puddings!

Materials
Oddments of deep green and pink DK yarns, or finer. Size 3¼mm needles.

Leaves
Using green yarn loosely cast on 20sts. Work in single rib for 3 rows.
Row 4: (k2 tog) 10 times.
Gather the sts on to a wool needle, threading the needle twice through the sts, then draw up tightly. Leave a tail long enough to sew the leaf to the stalk. Darn in the other end.
The size of the leaves can be varied by casting on more of fewer sts and working more or fewer rows.

Stalks
Using pink yarn, cast on 7sts and knit one row. Cast off, leaving a tail of about 10cm (4in) and use this to sew the cast on and off edges together to make a narrow tube. Tie the two ends together and leave them hanging.
Using the green tail from the leaf, sew the stalk to the leaf centre and darn in the end. Use the pink tails to sew the stalks firmly to the garden plot in a bunch. To keep the stalks and leaves upright, it may be necessary to stitch the leaves together here and there.

STRAWBERRY BED
Cottage gardens

Use small amounts of bright green DK yarn and bright red for embroidered berries. Size 4mm needles.
Cast on about 7sts and knit a strip of g st as long as required. Embroider this with a speckling of bright red tiny stitches and then stitch the strip down on to the plot.

Foliage, plants and flowers

FOLIAGE AND PLANTS

The following coloured patterns are simple to work and will prove very useful in your garden.

1. Slip-stitch plants, using greens on neutral and brown. This is a simple slip-stitch pattern in stocking stitch. Although two colours make the pattern, only one yarn is used at a time so this is much easier than intarsia patterns, where one yarn has to be carried across the back.

   Worked on a multiple of 4sts plus 3.

   Row 1: (RS) with brown, knit.

   Row 2: purl.

   Row 3: with green, k1, *sl 1, k3, * to last 2sts, sl 1, k1.

   Row 4: p1, *sl 1, p3* to last 2sts, sl 1, p1.

   Rows 5 and 6: as rows 1 and 2.

   Row 7: with green, k3, *sl 1, k3* to end of row.

   Row 8: p3, *sl 1, p3* to end of row.

   Repeat these 8 rows, using various browns and greens.

2. Tiny seedlings, using green on neutral, (or any brown for the earth). This is a simple slip-stitch pattern in which alternate sts are slipped purlwise, (p-wise), that is, with the yarn at the front and the needle going into the front of the stitch.

   Worked on a multiple of 2sts plus 1.

   Rows 1, 2, 5 and 6: with neutral or brown, knit.

   Row 3: green, *k1, sl 1 p-wise*, k1.

   Row 4: green, *k1, y fwd, sl 1 p-wise, y bk* k1.

   Row 7: green, *sl 1 p-wise, k1* sl 1.

   Row 8: green, *sl 1 p-wise, y bk, k1, y fwd* sl 1.

   Repeat these 8 rows.

3. Small bobbles, using two greens to look like close growth.

   Worked on a multiple of 4sts plus 2 but this stitch contracts, so allow plenty of sts.

   Row 1: (RS) with light green yarn, purl.

   Row 2: k1, *(k1, p1, k1) into next st, p3 tog.* to last st, k1.

   Row 3: with dark green yarn, purl.

   Row 4: k1, *p3 tog, (k1, p1, k1) into next st,* to last st, k1.

   Repeat these 4 rows. Change greens only on rows 2 or 4. Check every so often to see that you have the same number of sts on every row. Seen at an angle, this stitch is very convincing as a bed of plants.

4. Bobbles, using green yarn on a neutral background. Worked on any number of stitches, there are 4 clear sts between each bobble.

   To make a bobble, use green and increase five stitches into one, (i.e k, p, k, p, k into one st), then work backwards and forwards on these 5sts only in moss st, (or any other), for 3 rows. Then, with RS facing, (k2tog) twice, and pass one st over the top of the other one, knit the 5th st, and pass the other st over the top of it.

As you knit the next four sts, (in neutral), weave the green yarn in behind, and work at least three plain rows between each bobble row.

5. Cut loops, and uncut loops, see fur stitch, page 121.

BORDER PLANTS, FLOWERS AND FOLIAGE

These simple methods give a very realistic effect and are useful for filling spaces in your garden.

1. This is an ideal way to use up odd lengths of yarn. It creates a good impression of low foliage, either in rows or at random, and is easy enough for a pair of small hands to make.

   Take a thick bundle of yarn, I used 6 to 8 strands of various greens and multi-colours, (textured ones are good for this), and place them side-by-side in a rope. Begin at one end and tie overhand knots along the entire length leaving a space of about 4cm (1½in) between each one. Pull each knot very tightly. Now cut the yarn between each knot so that you have a pile of tiny tied bundles, like the one at the top of the page.

   Thread a large pointed needle with a long length of matching smooth yarn and tie a tiny loop in the end. Thread the bundles, like beads, on to the yarn and slide each one down to the end, either pushing them together or leaving a space between. The needle should go through the centre of the knot at any angle. When the row is long enough for your purpose, do not break the yarn but pin it in place and sew it down with the same yarn and needle. When you reach the end, pass the needle through the tiny loop and finish off underneath.

   Alternatively, the bundles can just as easily be sewn down individually at random wherever they are needed, especially in window-boxes.

2. Low-growing plants. Using two strands of any type of yarn, one smooth and one textured, work on a thick needle size 5 or 6mm. Cast on as many stitches as you need to reach across the row, then cast off again. The textured bumps in the yarn will tend to fall only on one side of this cord and this will be the side to show on the surface of the garden. Sew it in place with matching yarn.

   A wider version of this can be made by knitting one or two rows and pushing the bumps through to one side.

3. Knitted picot-point chain, see seedlings on page 92.

4. Crochet zig-zag braid. Made by using 2 different green yarns together.

   Make a chain of 4, dc into first ch st made, this makes a loop, then * work 4 more ch and work a dc into the first of these 4 on the opposite side to the previous one*. Repeat from * to * for as long as needed.

   Note: the US equivalent of dc is single crochet.

TEXTURED FOLIAGE AND FLOWERS

Mostly these are made from pom-pons of alls sizes. Have a large supply handy so that you can use these immediately for bushes, potted shrubs, 'gap-fillers' and border plants.

Used in groups, just tie their cords together to keep them close and glue or sew in position. If sewn, the two ties can be taken through into the background, a little way apart and tied together underneath.

SEEDLINGS

For a continuous length of new-looking plants, a row of creeping nasturtiums or other low line of flowers, use a picot-point chain. This is not crochet but knitting, and easy enough for a child to undertake.

Simply cast on 4sts and immediately cast off 3 of them in the usual way. Now change the needle over, (with the one remaining stitch on it), from the RH to the LH and cast on three more sts to make another set of 4. Continue to cast off three and cast on three to produce a length of bumps as long as you need.

Variations

1. Use doubled or trebled yarns of different types and textures, and colours.
2. Change one of these yarns every few bumps for more variation. Just cut one off and tie another one in.
3. Use the quicker loose cast on method.
4. Use a glitter/metallic yarn here and there.
5. Use any size needles, but a 4mm needle will take 3 strands of DK quite easily. Try finer yarns too.
6. Spiral these lengths round to create an irregular look for flowers.
7. Straight ones will look more like formal rows of seedlings.
8. Sew them down, (or glue them), by first pinning the length in position and then stitching between each plant with the colour of the background.

TALL PLANTS GROWING ON CANES IN POTS
Friary gardens

These include tomatoes, beans, passion-flowers, and fuschias.

Measurements

About 14cm (5½in) high, or shorter. The pattern for the plant pot can be found on page 73.

Materials

Oddments of green yarns in any thickness used double, size 3.00 or 4.00mm crochet hook, or knitting needles as for seedlings.

For the cane, a length of fine wooden dowelling or doubled wire, stiff card for discs, padding and glue. Fine pliers and wire cutters will be needed if using wire.

Basic pattern

1. First make a large plant pot and cut two card discs, one for the base and one for the topsoil. The diagram, see Fig 1, shows how these are attached to the support.
2. Cut a length of fine dowelling, or use an old wooden knitting needle, about 14cm (5½in) long or, if you are using wire, double this length and then fold it over with the loop at the top. See No 4 for this.
3. The diagram shows how this support is pushed through a hole in the centre of the small disc, which is then glued to the inside base. Then the padding is put on top, and then the soil disc. These are then pushed down into the pot and glued in place. Use the points of scissors to push the padding down firmly round the support, before lowering the soil disc.

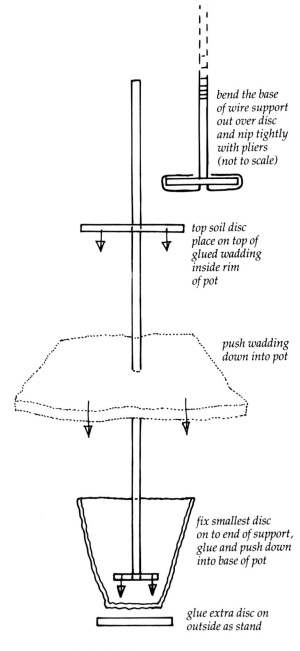

bend the base
of wire support
out over disc
and nip tightly
with pliers
(not to scale)

top soil disc
place on top of
glued wadding
inside rim
of pot

push wadding
down into pot

fix smallest disc
on to end of support,
glue and push down
into base of pot

glue extra disc on
outside as stand

fig 1 **tall plants on canes**

4. If wire is used instead of wood, this must first be wrapped with yarn. Begin by wrapping the opened-out fold in the centre, then fold the wire tightly with the pliers and continue to wrap down the doubled length. Finish wrapping about 2.5cm (1in) from the ends and seal the yarn in place with sticky-tape.

5. Now push this end through the tiny disc of card with about 1cm (½in) of bare wire showing. Use the pliers to bend these two ends of wire in opposite directions, out and over the top of the card disc as shown in the diagram. Nip these ends tightly on to

the card with pliers. The disc can now be glued into the base of the pot.

6. With the topsoil disc of card glued in place and the edges of the knitting pulled over it, you are now ready to make the foliage. This can best be described as a 'scrumble' of either knitting or crochet and really defies description, except to say that any mess you can make, (or have already made!), with green oddments will be ideal! For anyone who cannot use a crochet hook, the best thing is to make a string of seedlings, see page 91, and wrap these round the support or simply make a messy-looking piece of knitting, wider at one end, and twist this round rather untidily.

7. For those who can crochet, even if only basically, my examples were made by crocheting a very messy jumble of stitches, wider at the base, with picots here and there, tailing off into a single chain. This was then spiralled round the support, and the two ends of the double yarn were then criss-crossed downwards over the top to hold the knitting/crochet in place.

PATCHES OF FLOWERS FOR HERBACEOUS BORDERS
Cottage gardens

These are tiny hummock-shaped domes of bright coloured flower heads set into card bases, seen in the cottage gardens. Knitted and padded. The oval card-shape needed for the base is about as big as a teaspoon. Use double DK yarns, or trebled 3plys, brightly-coloured oddments and greens, and quite thick needles, about 4½mm or larger.

Cast on about 5 to 7sts and knit a square piece. Cast off and pad slightly, placing the card piece on this and gathering the edges with a running stitch. Stitch across the back until all is secure, then glue this shape on to the border, or sew it.

Above: Close-up of the row of sweet peas in the cottage garden.

SWEET PEAS
Cottage gardens

A row of sweet peas is a delight and these are seen in the cottage garden.

Measurements
13 × 9.5cm (5 × 3¾in).

Materials
Stiff card to the above measurements, glue. Small amounts of green, white and coloured DK yarns and size 3¼mm needles.

Card foundation
To make the foundation, score lightly along the length of the card and fold it over to make a V-shape. Fold a tiny piece of card and glue this into the inside fold to keep the V open like a narrow tent.

Knitted cover
Cast on 24sts and work in ss for 6 rows. Continue in ss but on rows 7 and 11, k2tog at each end to make 20sts. Continue as before until 17 rows have been worked.
Row 18: knit instead of purl.
Continue as before, in ss.
Row 24 and 28: inc at each end of these 2 rows. Continue in ss for 6 more rows, then cast off.

Making up
Fold this piece along the rev ss row and sew up the 2 sides. Glue this cover in place on the card foundation and embroider sticks and flowers using white and coloured yarns as shown.

WATER LILIES
Cottage gardens

These blooms can be placed on the pond in the cottage garden.

Materials
Use very tiny amounts of green and white, or pink yarns, DK or finer. Size 3¼mm needles.

Flowers
With white or pink yarn cast on 10sts and work one row single rib.
Next row: (k2tog) 5 times.
Gather these sts on to a wool needle and draw up. Sew up the two short sides to form a cup and use the tail to sew this on to the surface of the pond.

Leaves
With green yarn cast on 16sts and work 2 rows single rib.
Next row: (k2 tog) 8 times.
Gather these sts on to a wool needle and draw up. Sew these in place on the pond.

Below: Water lillies float on the pond in the cottage garden.

APPLIQUÉ SUNFLOWER
House pillow

Appliqué is used for this version.

Materials
Two different bright yellow oddments of DK yarns also oddments of green and brown, with brick-red for the plant pot. Size 3¼mm needles.

Basic pattern

Make the centre of the flower first. With brown yarn, cast on 5sts and work in moss st for 10 rows. Cast off and fold this piece across the middle and sew on three sides to make a roundish pad.

With yellow yarn, make the petals as follows. Cast on 6sts, *then cast off 5 of them in the usual way, but knitting into the back of the last st before casting the previous one over it. Transfer the last rem st to the LH and cast on 5 more sts.*

Repeat from * to * until a length of 9 petals has been made. Finish off, see Fig 1.

fig 1 sunflower petals versions 1 and 2

Now do the same again with the second yellow yarn, then tie the tails together to form 2 circles of petals and leave the ends loose.

Place these rings of petals round the brown pad and sew all round from the back. They should fit more or less exactly without gathering. Darn ends in.

To make the leaves, use two or three different greens and make as many as required. Cast on 5sts with green and knit one row.

Row 2: inc in first and last sts to make 7.
Row 3: inc in first and last sts to make 9.
Row 4: cast on 2sts, cast off 2sts and k to end of row.
Row 5: k2tog at each end of the row.
Row 6: as row 5, (5sts), then cast off.

Thread the two ends of yarn, individually, into a wool needle and darn them down to the pointed end of the leaf. Leave them loose for sewing on, **.

Embroider a stem, and attach the sunflower head and leaves in position.

To make the plant pot, use the brick-red yarn, cast on 7sts and knit one row. Now work 3 rows of ss, beginning with a purl row.

Row 5: inc 1st at each end of row to make 7sts.
Rows 6 and 7: purl.
Row 8: knit, then cast off.
Sew the plant pot over the base of the stem.

SUNFLOWER
Friary gardens

Version 2 is seen growing in a tub in the friary garden. The sunflower and leaves are made in exactly the same way as version 1, from the beginning to **.

Materials required for the three-dimensional version include a length of stiff wire about 35.5cm (14in) long, fine pliers, three discs of card and a tube of card for the tub. Glue will also be needed, and sticky tape.

1. The stalk is made by folding the wire in half, wrapping the fold with yarn and continuing down the stem where the yarn is fixed with sticky-tape about 3cm (1¼in) from the end. Leave the rest of the wire bare.
2. Sew the flower head to the folded end of the stalk, then sew on the leaves, (about 8 of these), alternately down the stem, using the tails to do this.

Above: Close-up of the potted sunflower.

3. Use the card tube to make the outer rim of the tub, (a cut-off toilet roll is perfect). Cut out three discs of card just big enough to fit inside the tub sides. Trim one of them slightly smaller than the other two.
4. Fix one of them to the base with sticky-tape.
5. Make holes in the other two just large enough to pass the stem through, and slide the stem first into the larger disc and then into the smaller one.
6. Using the pliers, fold up the ends of the wires at right-angles, push the lower disc down on to these and then bend the wire over the top of the disc and squeeze down flat.
7. Glue the base of the disc and push it down to the bottom of the tub.
8. Now slide the upper disc, (the soil), on to the top of the tub to hold the stem in place. Glue lightly round the edge.
9. Now make a covering of knitting for the tub. If a toilet-roll is used for this, 29sts in DK yarn on size 4mm needles will be needed. Sew up the rectangle of knitting to make a tube and glue this in place on the tub. Pull the edges well up to cover the card.

Populating your garden

Every garden must be regularly tended to keep it
immaculate and many hands make light work.
A selection of agreeable companions is given in
this chapter, but children may wish to clothe them in
their own imagination, or identify with
their families. The figures can easily be adapted
by changing a detail here and there and make
delightful gifts in their own right.

Above: The smallest figures are seen in Cottage Row.

Smallest figures

Though tiny, these figures seen in the cottage gardens are not quite to the scale of the cottages, but that would have made things very difficult so I feel that few will mind the fault. They are still quite fiddly to make on fine needles with double DMC Broder Medici, which is a very fine pure wool thread sold in small skeins perfect for fine crochet or knitting. Used double, many other colours can be created by mixing one strand of each colour. The bodies have no wire frames but are padded with a synthetic padding so they can be washed, see Fig 1.

Measurements

9–10cm (3½–4in) tall.

Materials

Doubled very fine threads (see above), or similar, in flesh colours, brown for boots with any other colours for the clothes, in small amounts. One skein of DMC flesh colour will make several figures.

Padding is also needed and sizes 2¼mm, 3mm and 4mm needles.

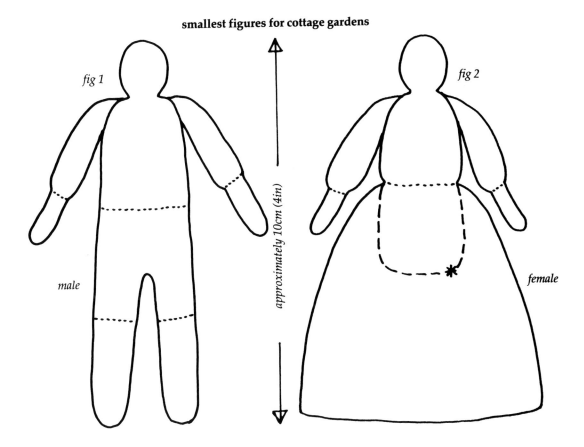

smallest figures for cottage gardens

fig 1

male

approximately 10cm (4in)

fig 2

female

Knitted cover

1. Begin at the top of the head with flesh colour used *double* throughout, unless a substitute is used. Cast on 10sts and work 8 rows in ss.
2. To shape the shoulders, change to shirt or blouse colour.
   Row 9: inc into every st to make 20sts.
   Row 10: inc into 1st, 10th, 11th and 20th sts to make 24sts.
   Continue to work in ss for 12 more rows.
3. To begin the trousers (or legs) for the male version, change to trouser colour and work 8 rows in ss. (** Cast off here for female version.)
4. Divide for the legs: work on the first 12sts for 6 rows and then change to leggings or boot colour and continue for 15 more rows. Do not cast off but gather the sts on to a wool needle and draw up to form the end of the foot.
5. Return to the other 12sts and work in the same way.
6. Sew up the head and pad firmly, then gather the neck tightly and stitch.
7. Continue to sew down the back as far as the waist and pad the upper body.
8. Sew the feet and leg seams and pad very gently without unduly stretching the fabric. Continue to sew and pad up towards the waist.
9. Complete padding and secure all threads. Squeeze gently into shape.

10. The upper arms are made in the same colour as either the jumper or the shirt, then change to flesh colour for the lower arms and hands, or you could work entirely in flesh colour. In the chosen colour, cast on 8sts and work in g st for 12 rows. Now change to flesh colour and ss and dec 3sts in the first row, to 5sts.
11. Work 10 rows in ss on these 5sts, then gather up as for the feet.
12. It is not necessary to pad the arms, just sew them up and attach to the shoulders with the seams underneath.

Waistcoat for men in shirtsleeves

This is made in three pieces.

1. Back: using double yarn, cast on 10sts and knit 16 rows. For the armholes, cast off 2sts at beg of next 2 rows. Work 6 more rows in g st. Cast off.
2. Fronts, both alike: cast on 4sts and knit 16 rows.
   Row 17: k2tog, k to end of row.
   Work 5 more rows in g st then cast off.
3. Sew up the shoulders and the side seams as far as the armholes. The waistcoat can be fastened in front with a few stitches, a button and loop, or a tie, or it can be left open.

Jumper (back and front alike)

1. Using coloured yarn, cast on 11sts and knit 20 rows. For the armhole, cast off 2sts at beg of next 2 rows. Work in g st for 6 more rows. Cast off. Make another piece the same.
2. Sew up the side seams and shoulders, leaving room for the head. For the arms, see Nos 10, 11 and 12 under trousers.

Hair and features

Embroider the face using a pointed, (not blunt), needle and single thread. The hair can also be emboidered using long stitches, or it can be knitted as follows:– Cast on 10sts and knit about 8 or 9 rows g st. Do not cast off but gather the sts into a cup shape for the top of the head. Pull this well down on to the nape of the neck and sew in place with matching yarn.

Woman

The body is basically the same as the man's except that she has no legs, as these are hidden by her long skirt. As seen in the diagram Fig 2, knitting stops after the 8 rows of ss below the 'waistline' though the woman's waistline has actually been moved upwards a little. Do not change colour as for the trousers, but continue the body colour as far as ** and then cast off.

The long skirt is sewn on over the lower body as shown, moving the waist higher up than is shown on the man. This can be made in any colour or stitch variation, but basically consists of a rectangle measuring 13 × 6cm (5 × 2¼in). For this, use size 3mm needles. Sew up the back seam and stitch in place on the body.

As for the previous version, the hair can be embroidered or knitted, with an added topknot of gathered threads.

White shawl

Use single very fine yarn on size 4mm needles, cast on 14sts and work in g st for 3 rows. Dec one st at each end of next and every alt row until 2sts rem. Cast off.

Apron

Using fine white yarn and size 2¼mm needles, cast on 10sts and work in ss for 10 rows.
Row 11: (k2tog) 5 times, then cast off.
Make a crochet chain or twisted cord and attach this to each side of the top edge. Tie on to the figure.

Straw hat (for man or woman)

Use straw-coloured yarn and size 3mm needles. Cast on 30sts in the loose cast on method. K4 rows.
Row 5: (k2tog) 15 times.
Rows 6 and 8: purl.
Rows 7, 9 and 10: knit.
Gather the last 15sts on to a wool needle and draw up to form the top of the hat. Leave a tiny hole. Sew the crown as far as the first ss row, then run a gathering

thread round this row to draw the hat in for a close fit. Sew the brim then stitch the hat to the head.

Extras

Other accessories could include a headscarf, basket, bunch of flowers, buttons and beads, frilled collar or parasol. Or give one of your figures a tiny plant pot to hold, or a vegetable for the kitchen.

The Dove family

These delightful characters are just the right size for the bedspread garden, Dove Cottage and the friary garden. Their names are John, Amy, Prudence, Sally and the children, Peter and Lovey, see illustrations on page 103. I have not yet been able to work out quite how they are related to each other, but perhaps you will get to know them better than I do and discover for yourself!

The figures are made on finer-than-usual needles with DK yarn to produce a dense and firm fabric which will not allow the padding to peep through. If thicker needles are used then, naturally, a larger figure will result with a more open texture and for young or old fingers, this may be easier to knit.

The three basic types are adaptable to all your own ideas and should be regarded as starting points for your imagination, see Fig 1. Add headscarves, jackets and other details to make each one different, or create your favourite story characters, gnomes and dwarves.

JOHN DOVE

John stands a little taller than the rest of the figures and is knitted in one piece.

Measurements
Approximately 19cm (7½in) tall.

Materials
Oddments of flesh colour for face and hands, other oddments for trousers, shirt and waistcoat, hair and boots.
Sizes 2¼mm, 3¼mm and 4mm needles. Padding.

Knitted cover

1. Legs and lower body: with boot-coloured yarn, cast on 14sts and knit 7 rows.
   Row 8: purl.
   Continue in ss for 5 more rows.
   Row 14: knit.
   Change to trouser colour and work 20 rows in ss. Purl one row and cast off. Work another piece in same way.

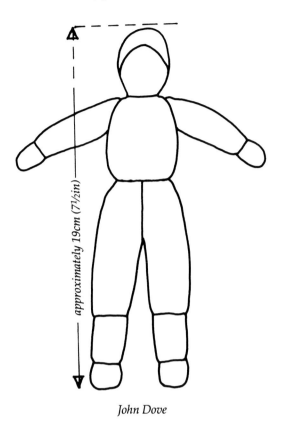

fig 1 **Dove family**

John Dove

2. Lay these 2 pieces with RS tog and stitch down from the waist to the top of the boots. Do this on both edges and leave the threads hanging.
3. Fold across the waistband to separate the legs and sew each inside leg as far as the top of the boots.
4. Sew across the bottom of the foot, then the inside boot edge. Complete the other leg in the same way. Turn to the RS.
5. Pad the legs and lower body but not too tightly. Run a gathering st of boot-coloured yarn round the top of the garter st foot and draw up slightly.
6. Upper body and head: with shirt-coloured yarn and size 2¼mm needles, cast on 26sts and knit 19 rows.
   Row 20: (k2tog, k10) twice, k2tog.
   Change to flesh-coloured yarn for head and work in ss for 12 rows. Gather these sts on to a wool needle and draw up to form the top of the head.
7. Sew down the head towards the neck. Change to shirt colour and sew down to the waist. Pad the upper body and sew round the two edges to attach the upper and lower sections of the body.
8. Sleeves and hands: using the same needles and shirt colour, cast on 13sts and knit 14 rows.
   Row 15: (k2, k2tog) 3 times, k1, (10sts).
   Change to pink yarn and work in ss, beg with a knit row, for 6 rows.
   Next row: (k2tog) 5 times.

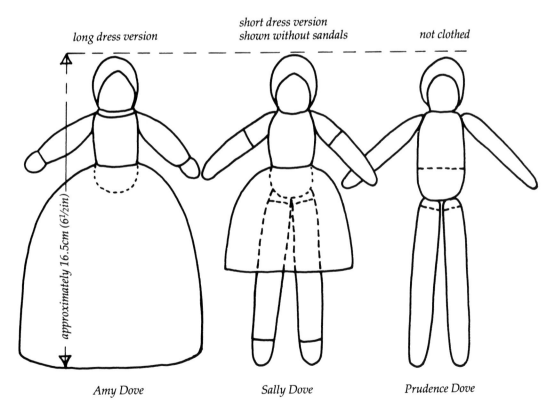

long dress version

short dress version
shown without sandals

not clothed

Amy Dove

Sally Dove

Prudence Dove

Gather the last 6sts on to a wool needle and draw up tightly. Sew up the arm as far as the shirt, then change colour and sew the shirt sleeve.
Make another piece in the same way.

9. The hair: using size 2¼mm needles and hair-coloured yarn, use the loose cast on to make 20sts and knit 8 rows.
Row 9: (k3, k2tog) 4 times.
Row 10: purl.
Gather the last sts on to a wool needle and draw up tightly. Sew up the sides to form a cup shape and fit this on to the head. Sew all round then, with the same yarn, extend stitches down from the hairline on to the face and neck as shown.

Waistcoat or jerkin

This is worked in three pieces.
Back: using size 4mm needles, and an oddment of coloured yarn, cast on 14sts and work 2 rows in single rib. Change to ss and work 8 rows. Cast off 2sts at the beg of the next 2 rows. Continue on these 10sts for 6 more rows.
Next row: (k1, p1) 5 times. Cast off in rib.
Right front: [note: knit the first and last sts in *every* row.] Cast on 8sts and work 2 rows in single rib.
Change to ss and work 9 rows. Cast off 2sts at beg of the next row, p to end. Continue on rem 6sts for 6 more rows.
Next row: (k1, p1) 3 times. Cast off in rib.
Left Front: cast on 8sts and work 2 rows in single rib. Change to ss and work 8 rows. Cast off 2sts at beg of next row and k to end. Continue on rem 6sts for 7 more rows, then finish off as for right front.
Attach at shoulders half-way across each front shoulder edge. Sew up the 2 side seams and press gently under a damp cloth. Sew buttons or beads down the right front.

AMY DOVE

This version features a long dress and the pieces are knitted separately

Measurements

Approximately 16.5cm (6½in) tall.

Materials

Approximately 25gm (1oz) DK yarn for the dress and oddments of pink DK for the head and hands. Hair-coloured yarn.
Padding. Size 3¼ and 2¼mm needles.

Body and head

Using size 2¼mm needles and dress-coloured yarn, cast on 22sts and work 16 rows in ss.
Row 17: purl.
Row 18: change to pink yarn and purl one row.
Continue in ss for 11 more rows.

Do not cast off, but gather the sts on to a wool needle and draw up to form the top of the head. Using the same thread, sew the head as far as the neck, then change yarns and sew down the body to the base.
Pad the head space and gather the neck gently with pink yarn just above the purl row of the bodice colour. Pad the body space and lace across the opening to keep the padding in place.

Sleeves and hands

Using the same yarn and needles as for the bodice, cast on 10sts and work in g st for 16 rows. Change to pink and work 4 rows in ss. Shape for the hand:
Row 5: (k2tog) 5 times.
Gather the rem sts on to a wool needle and sew up the hand from the WS. Change yarn colour and sew up the sleeve. Turn to RS, pad gently and attach to body at shoulders.

Long skirt

Using size 3¼mm needles and same yarn as bodice, cast on 25sts and work in g st for 16cm (6¼in). Cast off and sew the two short edges together. Turn to RS and gather one edge of the tube, then sew this around the waist of the figure, allowing at least 12 rows of the bodice to appear above. Make a cord or plait and tie this in a bow around the waist, or make an apron.
This figure will stand quite firmly on the edges of the skirt, but legs can be made for it, if you prefer. It may also be padded and sewn up to make the skirt completely solid, with a card base attached to the bottom edge, as illustrated here.

Hair and features

Using hair-coloured yarn and size 2¼mm needles, cast on 16sts and work 10 rows in g st. Change to ss and work 6 more rows.
Gather the last row on to a wool needle and draw up to make a cup shape. Sew about 6mm (¼in) down from the centre to close the gap at the crown. Fit this piece on to the head pulling the back well down on to the neck. Stitch all round. Use either the smooth or the rough side of this piece.
Embroider the features with fine yarn or stranded cotton.

Opposite: Members of the Dove family are seen tending their large garden.

SALLY DOVE

This version features a short dress and the pieces are knitted separately.

Measurements

Approximately 16.5cm (6½in) tall.

Materials

Approximately 25gm (1oz) pink DK for body, 25gm (1oz) dress colour, oddments for hair, white for pants and brown for sandals.
Sizes 2¼ and 3¼mm needles and some padding.

Body and head

Using size 2¼mm needles, and white yarn, cast on 22sts and work 9 rows in ss.
Row 10: knit.
Change to dress-coloured yarn and work 9 rows in ss.
Row 20: knit.
Change to pink yarn and work in ss for 14 rows.
**Do not cast off but gather the sts on to a wool needle and draw up to form the top of the head. Run the needle twice through the sts and pull tightly, then sew down the head as far as the neck. With matching colours, sew the rest of the body from the WS and turn to RS.
Place padding inside the head-end of this piece and run a gathering thread of pink yarn round the neck, two complete rows above the top of the bodice. Draw up gently to form the neck and fasten off.
Place padding in the rest of the body and sew the bottom edges together.

Legs

The feet and sandals are added later. Using white yarn, cast on 12sts and knit 2 rows.
Change to pink yarn and continue in ss for 29 rows, beg with a purl row.
Gather the last row on to a wool needle and draw up tightly. On the WS sew up the two side edges as far as the top of the leg. Turn to the RS and pad firmly but not too tightly. Gather the top edges together very slightly while at the same time sewing them across the top with the seam at the back centre. The leg should be stitched from the front *and* the back so that it remains flexible at this point. Stitch the leg to the body and gather round the ankle. Make another leg in the same way.
This is the barefoot version: two alternatives are to change to shoe-coloured yarn on the last 4 rows or to make separate shoes like those of the friars. The same pattern can be used. Sandal pattern will be found at the end of this section on Sally Dove.

Arms

Using dress-coloured yarn, cast on 10sts and work 5 rows in ss.
Row 6: knit.

Change to pink yarn and work in ss for 12 rows.
Next row: (k2tog) 5 times.
Gather the sts on to a wool needle and draw up to form the end of the hand. Make a second arm in the same way.
Alternatives include using g st instead of ss, making long or three-quarter sleeves or making full sleeves which decrease to 5sts at the wrist.
Sew the hands and arms, pad gently, fold across and sew on to the body at the shoulders as shown.

Skirt

Using size 3¼mm needles and dress-coloured yarn, cast on 48sts and work in ss for 5 rows, moss st for 2 rows, and ss for 13 rows, (20 rows in all). Cast off.
[Note: the pattern for this may be varied.]
Sew up the two short sides then gather the top edge and draw up to fit the waist round the bodice. Sew this piece on to the bodice, taking care to hide the white stitches below the waist. Embroider the face.
The hair is made in the same way as Amy's.

Sandals

These consist of pink foot sections and brown soles with straps. Using size 3¼mm needles and brown yarn, cast on 14sts and knit 2 rows.
Row 3: change to pink yarn and purl one row, weaving brown ends in as you go.
Row 4: knit.
Row 5: cast off 3sts p-wise, p to end.
Row 6: cast off 3sts and k to end.
Gather the last 8sts on to a long thread and leave. Fold the piece in half and from the RS sew up the brown edges, first stitching upwards on to the toe of the sandal then continuing towards the fold, (at the back of the foot). Place this piece on to the foot of the figure with the gathered stitches round the back of the ankle. Hold in place with a pin.
Push a tiny piece of padding into the toe end, squeeze the top edges together and sew the top of the foot neatly, pulling the edges together from side to side as you go. Push the needle back towards the leg and stitch the gathered stitches on to the ankle.
Make a strap from a brown crochet chain, or make a cord or plait instead. This is then sewn over the top of the foot at a slight angle as shown. Make another one in the same way.

PRUDENCE DOVE

This version features a long dress and the pieces are knitted separately.

Measurements

Approximately 16.5cm (6½in) tall.

Materials

Approximately 25gm (1oz) pink DK for body, and

oddments for dress, white pants, hair and sandals.
Sizes 2¼ and 3¼mm needles, and some padding.

Body, head and legs

Using size 2¼mm needles and white yarn, cast on 22sts and work 9 rows in ss.
Row 10: knit.
Change to pink yarn and continue in ss for 24 rows. Complete as instructions for Sally Dove from **. The legs are also made in the same way. The neck should be gathered on the 10th row from the top.

Arms

Using pink yarn and the same needles, cast on 8sts and work in ss for 22 rows.
Next row: (k2tog) 4 times.
Gather the last sts on to a wool needle to form the end of the hand. Sew the arms, from the WS along the edges, then turn to RS, pad gently, fold across the tops and sew to the shoulder line of the body.
Make the hair and the sandals in the same way as Amy's and Sally's.

Long sleeveless dress

With size 3¼mm needles, cast on 42sts. Work 4 rows in moss st.
Row 5: (k2, p2) 10 times, k2.
Row 6: (p2, k2) 10 times, p2.
Work 28 more rows in this double rib.
Row 33: (k2tog, p2) 10 times, k2tog, (31sts).
Row 34: (p1, k2tog) 10 times, p1, (21sts).
Row 35: purl.
Row 36: k11, turn and work on these 11sts for 6 rows in ss. Cast off. Join yarn to rem 10sts and complete in same way.
Fold in half with WS tog, and sew side seam as far as armhole. The seam will run down one side of the dress, not the centre back. Turn to RS and fit on to the figure, then stitch across each shoulder and darn ends in.

Hat

This should be measured over the knitted hair, so if your figure is different in this respect you may have to adjust the number of stitches accordingly.
Using white yarn, and size 3¼mm needles, cast on 22sts.
Rows 1, 3, 4 and 5: knit.
Row 2: purl.
This section completes the crown; thread these sts on to a wool needle and draw up tightly for the top of the hat.
For the brim, cast on 46sts and knit 3 rows.
Row 4: (k2tog, k2) 11 times, k2tog, (34sts).
Row 5: (k2tog, k1) 11 times, k1, (23sts).
Cast off and sew the two side edges tog. Matching the two seams, sew the brim to the crown from the inside.

THE CHILDREN, PETER AND LOVEY DOVE

The boy and girl body-shapes are exactly the same, including white knitted-in pants; only the outer clothes are different. Basically they are made in the same way as Prudence, with separate clothes but this can easily be adapted to a built-on clothes design, like John and Amy. The trouble is that on this small scale, although it is more fun to be able to remove and change the clothes, the figures tend to look rather podgy and over-fed unless they are padded very sparingly!

Measurements

14cm (5½in) tall.

Materials

Oddments of pink DK yarns, white, hair-colour, clothes colours and shoes.
Sizes 2¼, 3¼ and 4mm needles and some padding.

Body

Beginning with the pants, use white yarn and size 2¼mm needles. Cast on 18sts and work 8 rows in ss. Change to pink yarn and work 20 more rows.
Gather the last row on to a wool needle and draw up for the top of the head.

Legs

Using white yarn, cast on 10sts and work 4 rows in ss. Change to pink yarn and continue for 16 more rows. Change to brown yarn for the shoes and knit the next three rows in g st, then work in ss for three rows. Gather the last row on to a wool needle to form the end of the foot.
Make the second leg in the same way.

Arms

With pink yarn, cast on 8sts and work in ss for 16 rows. Gather the last row on to a wool needle for the end of the hand. Make two the same.

Making up

From the WS sew up the main body piece and turn to the RS. Gather the neck 12 rows down from the top of the head. Pad the head area then pull the gathered sts tightly and finish off securely. Pad the body area, (not too much!), and sew across the bottom.
Sew up the leg seams from the WS, turn to the RS and pad. Using white yarn, attach the legs to the base of the body. Do the same with the arm pieces, sewing them on to the shoulders just below the gathered neck.

Hair

Using size 3¼mm needles and hair-coloured yarn, cast on 16sts.
Rows 1, 2, 4 and 6: knit.
Rows 3 and 5: purl.

Row 7: cast on 3sts, p19, working into the back of the 4th st.
Row 8: (k1, p2tog) 6 times, k1.
Row 9: purl.
Gather the last sts on to a wool needle and draw up for the top. Fit the cap of hair on to the head and sew in place. The reverse side can also be used and stitch patterns can be changed as required.

Trousers

Using size 3¼mm needles and brown yarn, cast on 12sts and knit 3 rows.
Row 4: purl.
Rows 5 to 19: ss, (lengthen or shorten at this stage).
Row 20: knit.
Cast off and make another piece in the same way. To make up, lay the two pieces RS tog and sew one-third of the way down from the top edge. Fold the pieces so that the seams lie at front and back with the legs divided. Now sew from one ankle along both inside legs down to the other ankle.
To make the bib and straps, cast on 6sts and knit 8 rows. Ease this shape into a square and sew it on to the front edge of the trousers. Make a crochet cord to go from one corner down to the centre back and over to the other corner, sewing this on to the trousers at the three points.

One-piece shirt

Using size 3¼mm needles and white yarn, cast on 12sts and knit 2 rows.
Row 3: purl, and continue in ss for 6 more rows.
Row 9: cast on 5sts and k across all 17sts.
Row 10: cast on 5sts and p across all 22sts.
Rows 11 and 12: ss.
Row 13: k8, cast off 6sts, k8.
Row 14: p8.
Row 15: cast on 3sts, k11, turn and work on these 11sts for 4 more rows.
Row 20: cast off 5sts p-wise, p to end of row, (6sts). Work in ss for 7 more rows.
Row 28: knit.
Row 29: cast off p-wise.
Cut yarn and rejoin to second set of 8sts.
Row 30: p8.
Row 31: k8.
Row 32: cast on 3sts, p11.
Now continue in ss for 4 rows.
Row 37: cast off 5sts and k to end of row, (6sts).
Now continue in ss for 7 more rows.
Row 45: p.
Cast off.
To make up, fold the piece with RS tog, and use the cast on and cast off tails to sew up the side and sleeve seams. Turn to RS and fit this on to the figure. There are no fastenings on the shirt; tuck it into the trousers and open out the front neck.

Dress

Using dress-coloured yarn and size 4mm needles, cast on 40sts for the skirt and bodice. Work 3 rows in moss st, then continue in ss for 8 rows, beg with a knit row.
Row 12: (k1, k2tog) 13 times, k1, (27sts).
Row 13: purl.
Change to size 3¼mm needles and work 4 rows of ss. Now divide for the armholes.
Row 18: k7, turn and work in g st on these 7sts for 8 rows, then cast off.
Rejoin yarn to left over sts and k13. Turn, and work in g st for 8 rows, then cast off. Rejoin yarn to last 7sts and complete in the same way.
For the sleeves lay the piece out flat, RS uppermost, and pick up 13sts, (i.e 6sts down each side of the g st edge of the armhole and one at the base) to extend the sleeve. If you prefer, you can cast on 12sts and knit the sleeves separately, but picking up sts saves time and is less fiddly! Work in g st for 12 rows, then cast off and work the other sleeve in the same way.
To make up, fold the piece with RS tog and sew up the back opening from hem to neck. Sew along the sleeve edges, leaving the neck area open at this stage. Turn to the RS.
Slip the garment over the head of the figure and stitch across the shoulders to close up the neck. The seam should be placed at the back.

The gardening friars

All year round the friars busily tend the garden to ensure supplies of fresh fruit, vegetables, herbs and honey. The small flower garden must be kept in trim too, for this is not only where the bees gather pollen but also where the brothers can rest from their labours and watch 'Mother Nature' at work, see illustration opposite.

Brother Francis feeds the birds and other small creatures during the colder days, especially when berries are difficult to find and the ground is too hard to peck at. Gradually they come closer and closer until some are sitting on his head and shoulders, while others stand on his hands to feed.

Brother Robert's work is to look after the bees, for the only way of sweetening food is with honey. They live in hives made of straw, called 'skeps', which stand above the damp ground on low wooden benches. In autumn, as the days get shorter and colder, the bees will sleep inside the skeps until the warmer days of spring. Brother Robert is always very polite and gentle

Opposite: It is difficult to recognize individual friars but they all play their part in the garden.

with the bees and they allow him to remove the honey without stinging him, but he wears a hat just the same!

Brother David is the oldest friar and always wears *his* straw hat in the garden. He looks after the cold frame, pots seedlings, gathers fruit from the bushes and takes vegetables to the kitchen. He even does some gentle hedge-trimming and weeding when necessary. He always keeps some of the outer cabbage leaves for the pet rabbit.

Brother John is the youngest of the gardening friars and makes himself useful wherever he can, helping to keep the garden tidy and beautiful by digging and hoeing. Today, he helps Brother Andrew to keep the weeds down but they can always find a moment to stand and admire the birds which so tamely feed at the hands of Brother Francis.

Brother Andrew is the head gardener. Even though he is mainly responsible for the garden, he still finds time to do his share of the digging and hoeing. He will show Brother David which of the medicinal herbs are ready to be gathered and give him the choicest vegetables for the meal of the day.

BASIC FIGURES

The basic body for all the gardening friars is exactly the same.

Measurements

18cm (7in) tall with shoes on!

Materials

Small amounts of flesh-coloured DK yarns for the body, plus a small oddment of white for the underpants. For the habit, about 20gm (¾oz) brown, black or grey, and oddments of white for the girdle. The sandals may be brown or black. Tiny oddments of coloured yarn for the hair and face.
Size 3mm needles and some padding.

Body and head

Begin at the base of the body and work upwards towards the top of the head. Using white yarn, cast on 18sts and work 10 rows in ss. Change to flesh-coloured yarn and work 14 rows in ss.
Row 25: k2tog at beg and end of this row.
Continue in ss for 9 more rows, then gather the last row on to a wool needle and draw up the sts tightly for the top of the head.
Legs: (make two) cast on 9sts and work 24 rows in ss. Gather the last sts on to a wool needle and draw up for the foot.
Arms: (make two) cast on 8sts and work in ss for 18 rows.
Row 19: (k2tog) 4 times.
Gather the last 4sts on to a wool needle to form the hand.

Making up

Sew the head and body piece into a tube, see Fig 1. Pad the head section and run a gathering thread round the neck, (the top 9 rows), and tie of securely. Pad the rest of the body and sew up with matching yarn.
Sew the legs and arms, leaving one end open for padding. Pad gently without distorting the fabric, then sew up the ends. Now attach the arms and legs to the body with flesh-coloured yarn.

Habit

Using brown, black or grey DK yarn and size 3mm needles, cast on 36sts. Work 4 rows in moss st followed by 26 rows in ss, with a border of 4 moss sts at each end of the row.
Row 31: (k2tog, k4) 6 times.
Now work in ss for 5 more rows.
Row 37: k7, turn, and work on these 7sts for 8 more rows, keeping the border of moss st as before.
Leave these 7sts on a spare needle.
Join the yarn to the centre sts and work in ss on these 16sts for 8 rows.
Next row: (k2, k2tog) 4 times, (12sts).
Leave these 12sts on a spare needle.
Join the yarn to the last 7sts and work in ss for 8 rows, keeping the border of moss st as before.
Next row: purl across the 12 centre sts and the 7 side sts from the spare needles, keeping the moss st patt in the last 4sts.
Hood: work all sts in ss for 2 rows, keeping the 4 moss sts at each end.
Now dec one st at each end of every row until 4sts rem. Cast off p-wise.
Sleeves: cast on 19sts and work 4 rows in moss st.
Row 5: k2tog, k15, k2tog.
Continue in ss for 5 more rows.
Row 11: k2tog, k13, k2tog.
Cast off p-wise and make another sleeve in the same way.

Making up

With WS tog, fold each sleeve in half and sew the side edges tog to form a tube. Turn to RS.
From the RS of the gown, insert each sleeve into the armhole and sew in place.
With WS tog, pin the front bands of moss st together and sew the gown front as far as the end of the moss st leaving an opening for the neck.

Sandals or shoes

With dark brown yarn and size 3¾mm needles, cast on 14sts and knit 3 rows.
Row 4: purl, then cast off.
Fold, and sew up the short edges. Cut a piece of card as shown, see Fig 2, and push this into the base of the shoe. Glue in place with the seam at the back, then sew the complete shoe to the bottom of the leg.

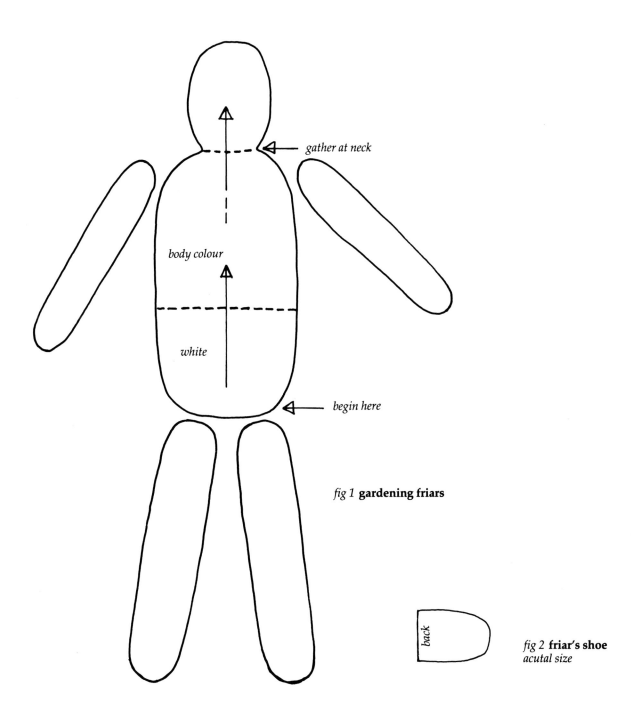

gather at neck

body colour

white

begin here

fig 1 **gardening friars**

back

fig 2 **friar's shoe**
acutal size

Girdle

Using white yarn, make a twisted cord or a plait measuring about 30cm (12in) long to tie round the waist. For Franciscan friars, who wear a brown habit, three knots should be tied in the ends of the girdle.

Straw hat

This is worn by Brother Robert and also by Brother David.

Materials

A small amount of straw-coloured DK yarn. Size 3¾mm needles.

Hat

For the crown, cast on 14sts and knit 4 rows.
Row 5: purl.
Row 6: knit.
Gather the sts on to a wool needle to form the top, then sew up the side edges.
To make the brim, cast on 36sts and knit 2 rows.
Row 3: (k2tog) 18 times.
Row 4: knit.
Gather the sts on to a wool needle to form a wide circle and sew the side edges together. Fit the brim round the edge of the crown and sew together.

Above: The birds and animals are frequent visitors to the gardens.

Animals and birds

SQUIRREL

As for the other tiny creatures, fine yarns are needed for the squirrel, either three strands of DMC Broder Medici used together, or any other 3 ply. He is quite a complex animal to make, and fiddly, but the result is a dear little chap who lends an authentic air to the larger gardens.

Materials

Small amounts of fine yarns, (as above), in dark and pale greys, some white and oddments of black and fawn for the features.
Size 2mm needles and some padding.
For a stand, a tiny oblong of stiff card. Small green bead.

Body

With grey yarn, cast on 16sts and work 6 rows of ss.
Row 7: dec one st at each end of the row.
Row 8: purl.
Row 9: k2tog, (k4, k2tog) twice.
Row 10: p11.
Rows 11 to 16: work straight in ss.
Row 17: k2tog, k2, k2tog, k3, k2tog.
Rows 18 to 20: ss on 8sts.
Row 21: (k2tog) 4 times.
Gather these sts on to a wool needle to form the top of the head.
With RS tog, sew up the body leaving a space at the lower end. Turn to RS and pad to form a tiny head and rounded lower body. Finish sewing up and gently

squeeze into shape. Run a gathering thread round the neck and finish off securely.

White front

With white yarn, cast on 4sts and work 6 rows of ss.
Row 7: inc one st at each end of row.
Rows 8, 9 and 10: ss.
Row 11: as row 7.
Rows 12 to 16: ss.
Row 17: k2tog at each end of row.
Rows 18, 19 and 20: ss.
Row 21: as row 17.
Rows 22, 23 and 24: ss.
Cast off, noting that this is the base of the white section. Sew this over the joining seam of the body with the top edge beginning just above the neck and the bottom edge underneath the base. Take care to keep it centred accurately.

Tail

Using pale grey yarn or a white and pale grey mixture, cast on 4sts and work 4 rows in ss. This is the flat base of the tail.
Row 5: inc in first st, k2, inc in last st.
Row 6: knit.
Continue to work in g st, increasing as before on rows 7, 9 and 11, (12sts).
Rows 12 to 20: knit.
Shape the top of the tail as follows:–
** **Row 21**: k6, turn and knit back to end of row.
Next row: k5, turn and knit back.
Continue in this way, knitting one less st on alternate rows until only one st has been knitted.
Knit across all sts to other end**, and rep from ** to **.
Next row: (k2tog) 6 times.
Next row: k6.
Gather these last sts on to a wool needle and draw up for the top curve of the tail. Use the same thread to sew down the tail from the RS, on the inside curve, (i.e nearest the squirrel's body), leaving the lower section open. Pad the tail section and pull into a curve as shown, but leave the lower end unpadded and open. Stitch the tail to the body with the smooth narrow part at the base lying flat on the back and the open part fitting the lower part of the back.

Front paws

With grey yarn, (as body), cast on 4sts and knit 6 rows. Gather the end, fold the piece in half and sew together. Sew the cast on edge to the shoulder, well up on the body. Make another in the same way.

Back legs

With same yarn, cast on 6sts and knit 8 rows.
Row 9: cast off 2sts at beg of row and knit to end.
Rows 10, 11 and 12: k4.

Gather the last sts on to a wool needle and fold the last 3 rows across to form a leg. Sew this as far as the wider part then fasten off. The wide end is left open and this is sewn on to the body over the lower section as shown.
The second leg is made in the same way except that the last three rows are folded over and sewn on the opposite side so that each leg has the seam on the inside.

Features

At the top of the head, use satin st to embroider over the extreme top edge of the white section to create a more pointed grey nose, then use fawn thread to embroider a tiny nose at the end of this.
The ears are made in grey yarn by making a vertical pile of satin stitches, (i.e on top of each other), until a little pointed extension develops. Darn ends in securely. The eyes are embroidered in black yarn or cotton. Make them fairly large as shown.
To help the squirrel keep his balance, make a small rectangle of stiff card and glue him on to this. His 'nut' is a bead glued between his paws.

RABBIT

Wild rabbit fur is a mixture of greys and browns, so your fine yarns should ideally be mixed in a triple-strand of two light browns and a pale grey. However, if you are using one 3 ply yarn instead of DMC Broder Medici, choose a brownish grey, or even white!
Our little friend is 5cm (2in) long so if you use thicker yarns your result will be a larger rabbit!

Materials

Fine yarn, (as above), in very small amounts of grey/brown, white and black.
Padding and size 2mm needles, also a pair of 2mm double-pointed needles.

Body

Cast on 12sts and work 2 rows of ss. This will be the tail end.
Row 3: inc in first st, k4, inc, k4, inc, k1.
Next and alt rows: purl.
Row 5: inc, k4, inc, k4, inc, k3, inc, (19sts).
Row 7: k9, inc, k9.
Rows 8 to 14: work in ss without shaping.
Row 15: (k2tog, k4) 3 times, k2tog.
Row 17: (k2tog, k2) 4 times.
Row 19: (k2tog, k2) 3 times.
Gather the last sts on to a wool needle and draw up to form the top of the body. Insert padding and also run a gathering thread through the cast on sts and draw up, then sew up. Squeeze into a plump oval.

Head

Cast on 8sts and work 2 rows in ss.
Row 3: inc in first st, k2, inc, k2, inc, k1.
Rows 4, 5 and 6: ss.
Row 7: (k2tog) 5 times, k1.
Row 8: p2, p2tog, p2.
Gather the last sts on to a wool needle and draw up tightly. Gather the other end, pad gently and sew up to make an oval. Sew the head on to the body as shown. Embroider the eyes with black yarn, and using satin stitch.

Vest

Using either a mixture, (in two strands), of grey and white fine yarns or white 3 ply alone, cast on 4sts and work 6 rows of ss.
Row 7: inc one st at each end to make 6sts.
Work 15 more rows of ss then cast off.
With the narrow end at the tail sew this strip on to the underside of the body with the cast off edge just underneath the chin.

Ears

With 2 strands of fine yarn in brown/grey, (as body), use double-pointed needles to cast on 3sts. Knit one row, then, *without turning the needle round* push the stitches to the other end of the needle and knit them, taking the yarn across the back of the stitches to do this. This will pull the two sides of the knitting together. Knit 4 rows altogether, then turn the needle round in the usual way (purl side facing) and cast off p-wise. Darn the cast on tail into the WS of the ear and use the other thread to sew the ear to the head. Make another ear in the same way.

Tail

Using brown and black fine yarns together, or black 3 ply alone, cast on 3sts and work 4 rows in ss. Change to white/grey, (or white alone), and work 4 more rows. Cast off.
Fold this piece across where the colours change and stitch up the sides. Sew this on to the rabbit with the black side uppermost at an upwards angle so that the white shows. Keeping it well under the body, stitch it to the base of the back in this position.

Back legs

Using body colour, follow the same instructions as for the squirrel.

Front legs

Using body colour, cast on 5sts and work 4 rows in ss.
Row 5: k2tog, k1, k2tog.
Row 6: p3.
Cast off and sew up from the cast on end as far as the 5th row, then leave the rest open. This part is to be sewn to the body, positioned well forward and low down to act as a support. Make the other one in the same way.

HEDGEHOG

The body is made from a pom-pon glued to an oval piece of card. It has a knitted head.

Materials

Oddments of fine mid and dark brown yarns for the body and pale brown or fawn for the head. A length of dark yarn for the eyes and nose.
Some padding and an oval of stiff card about 2cm (¾in) long for the base.
Size 2mm needles.

To make the hedgehog

Make a pom-pon measuring about 2cm (¾in) across using fine brown yarns. Trim it with scissors so that the underside is fairly flat and glue this to the oval of card.
To make the head: use pale brown or fawn yarn cast on 10sts and work 2 rows in ss.
Row 3: k2tog, k1, (k2tog) twice, k1, k2tog.
Rows 4 and 6: purl.
Row 5: (k2tog) 3 times.
Gather the last sts on to a wool needle to form the end of the nose. Sew up this piece to form a tiny cone shape and pad it slightly. Stitch across the end to hold the padding in place but *do not* pull the edges inwards. Embroider the eyes and nose with dark thread. Make a space in the pom-pon at a narrow end of the card and glue the head on to it. Trim neatly all round.

WOOD PIGEON OR DOVE

Fine yarns are required for this very small item and accurate padding and sewing is essential for a convincing shape and appearance. For best results, use double DMC Broder Medici or 2/3 ply knitting yarn in greys and white.
The birds are made in three parts so that the tail can become either narrow or wide and can be attached at any angle. The wings may also be shortened and sewn on in any position, open or closed.

Materials

Fine yarns, (see above), in greys and white, a very little padding for each bird, dark thread for eyes and light brown for beak.
Card for a stand, and size 2mm needles.

Body

Begin at the tail end with grey yarn and cast on 5sts.
Row 1: k.
Row 2: p.
Row 3: inc in first st, k3, inc in last st.
Row 4: p.
Continue to inc one st at each end of every knit row until there are 15sts.

Next row: p.
Work 8 more rows in ss.
Decrease one st at each end of the next 2 rows, (11sts).
Next row: k2tog, k2, k3tog, k2, k2tog.
Next row: p7.
Next row: k2tog, k3, k2tog.
Gather the last sts on to a thread and draw up to make the rounded head. Fold the piece to the wrong side and sew from the head end towards the tail, leaving a gap of about 1cm (½in) to turn the piece to the RS. Sew very accurately only into the edge stitches.
Turn to the RS and pad gently to obtain a plump breast and slender tail. Sew up the tail and darn the end in. Run a gathering thread round the neck and secure tightly. Embroider two large dark eyes and a beak.

Fan tail

Cast on 20sts in loose cast on method. For different widths of tail, this number can be varied between 10 and 20sts but decrease on row 9 accordingly. Work 8 rows in single rib.
Row 9: (k2tog) 10 times.
Row 10: *either* purl for a smooth line from body to tail *or* knit for a ridge at this point.
Cast off and run a gathering thread through this edge. Draw up securely. Sew this piece to the end of the body in an upright position, checking to see that this is placed centrally. See the underbody seam for this.

Wings

Make two the same. Cast on 5sts and knit 16 rows in g st.
Row 17: k1, sl 1, k1, psso, k2.
Rows 18, 19 and 20: knit 4.
Row 21: k1, sl 1, k1, psso, k1.
Rows 22, 23 and 24: knit 3.
Row 25: k1, sl 1, k1, pass 2sts over.
Darn in the yarn at the pointed end of the wing and use the other tail of yarn to attach the wings to the shoulders of the body along the top edges.

Smaller birds

All of the other species are based on the same pattern as the wood pigeon, except that the number of stitches and rows is varied.

1. Make the body shorter, same stitches, fewer rows.
2. Make the tail narrower and shorter.
3. Make the wings shorter, same stitches, miss out rows 19, 20, 23 and 24.
4. Vary the yarns too; change the colours of beaks and eyes and put an odd stripe in the wings and tail here and there, or a white collar round the neck. A thrush may have embroidered speckles on his breast and a robin may have an orange vest sewn on. Look in bird books for simple changes which you can make to the basic pattern. Can anyone knit an owl to scale?

Above: Two doves are shown on the house pillow, one free-standing and one in appliqué.

APPLIQUÉ DOVE
House pillow

This is made from two knitted shapes, see Fig 1, and is then sewn in place.

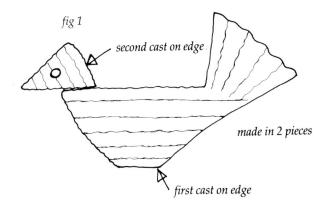

fig 1

second cast on edge

made in 2 pieces

first cast on edge

appliqué dove or wood pigeon

113

Materials

Oddments of pale grey and white DK yarns and size 3¼mm needles.

Body and tail sections

With grey yarn, cast on 5sts and knit one row.
Row 2: inc one st at each end of row, 7sts.
Rows 3 and 5: knit.
Row 4: inc one st at each end of row, 9sts.
Row 6: cast off 7sts and k the last one.
Row 7: inc in both sts to make 4sts.
Row 8: inc one st in first and last sts.
Row 9: (k1, p1) 3 times.
Row 10: inc in first st, (p1, k1) twice, inc in last st. Cast off in patt.

Head

With white yarn, cast on 4sts and knit 2 rows.
Row 3: (k2tog) twice.
Row 4: k2, then pass first st over 2nd to cast off.

Making up

Pin these two shapes to the roof of the house pillow in any position you wish and sew all round the edge with matching yarn.

Gardening teddy bears

'Why should humans have all the fun of the garden?' they say, so these two put on their special green garden clothes and are now all set to begin. For similar outfits for bears known to you personally, all you need are lots of oddments of green yarns, left over from other projects perhaps? A quick look at the diagrams, see Fig 1, will show how everything is made from either squares or oblongs, with very little shaping.

Although the clothes are removable for washing, there are a few fastenings, just ties and two button loops, but these will probably require the assistance of some human fingers to adjust!

The boy's outfit consists of a jumper, shorts, tool-apron and shoes. The girl's consists of a dress, panties, headscarf and shoes. As you will see, even the shorts are in different greens – just mix them all together freely for an interesting colour effect.

Measurements

To fit a 24cm (9½in) bear.

Materials

Total of approximately 150gm (5oz) of green DK yarns from assorted leftovers.
Size 3¾mm or 4mm needles.
Two small buttons for the dress.

Jumper

Two diagonal squares, plus two sleeves.
Cast on 2sts and knit them. Continue in g st.
Row 2: *inc one st at each end.
Row 3: knit. *
Repeat from * to * until there are 30sts, then change greens and knit one more row.
Now dec one st at each end of next and every alt row until only 2sts rem, then cast off.
Make another piece in the same way.
Make the sleeves as follows:– using 4 or 5 different greens to make stripes as required, cast on 24sts in one shade and work 2 rows in single rib.
Row 3: (k5, inc in next st) 4 times, (28sts).
Continue in ss for 17 rows beg with a purl row, and changing colours as you go. Cast off.

Making up

Attach the front and back squares at the shoulders with 2 or 3sts. Open the pieces out flat, lay the sleeves on top with RS together, and sew the sleeves in place along the armhole edges. Fold over, to place back and front together (RS tog) and sew the underarm and side seams. Turn to the RS.

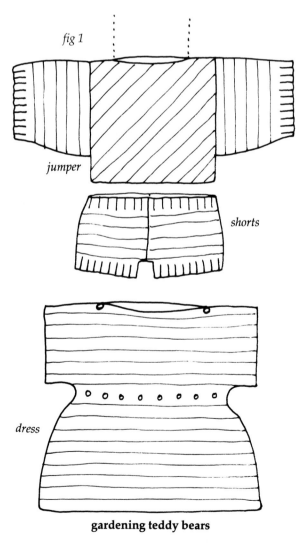

fig 1

jumper

shorts

dress

gardening teddy bears

Above: The clothes for the teddy bears can be made in any coloured oddments for a favourite toy.

Shorts

Made in two different greens.
Cast on 32sts and work in single rib for 2 rows.
Row 3: k2, (y fwd, k2tog, k1) to end of row.
This makes the holes for the waist cord.
Row 4: purl.
Work in ss for 10 rows.
Row 15: cast off 2sts and knit to end.
Row 16: cast off 2sts and purl to end.
Work 3 rows in single rib, then cast off in rib. Make another piece in the same way.

Making up

With RS together, fold each piece in half and sew up the lower three rows of ribbing and the three cast off stitches. This forms the two legs. Now join the two halves together down the centre front and centre back seams. Make a crochet chain or twisted cord and thread it through the holes.

Tool apron

Cast on 24sts and knit 2 rows. Continue in ss for 16 rows, beginning with a knit row.

Next row: purl.

Next row: knit.

Continue in rev ss for 7 more rows, then cast off. Now fold the piece up where the knitting changes from ss to rev ss, (the last 8 rows), and sew up the side edges to form a pocket. Place a few stitches in the centre to divide this section. Make two cords and attach these to each corner to tie round the waist.

Shoes

Made in two different greens. Work two in the same way.

For the soles, cast on 6sts and knit 2 rows.

Row 3: inc into first and last sts, (8sts).

Row 4: knit.

Row 5: as row 3, (10sts).

Continue in g st for 10 more rows.

Row 16: (k2tog) 5 times.

Row 17: knit.

Cast off.

For the uppers, cast on 7sts and work 13cm (5in) in moss st. Cast off.

Sew the two narrow edges together to form a tube, then sew one edge to the edge of the sole all the way round, positioning the back seam in the centre of the 5 cast off stitches of the sole.

Make cords to thread around the top edges of the shoes.

Dress

Use as many different shades of green as you wish. Cast on 45sts and work 2 rows in single rib. Work 18 rows of ss, placing stripes at random.

Row 21: k2 (k2tog, k2) 10 times, k2tog, k1.

Row 22: p34.

Row 23: (k1, y fwd, k2tog), to last st, k1, to make a row of holes.

Row 24: purl.

For the sleeves, cast on 6sts at beg of next 2 rows. Work in ss for 14 more rows, then cast off. Make another piece in the same way.

Making up

With RS together, sew the two pieces up the sides and underarms, then across the tops of the sleeves for 10sts only. Leave the rest open for the neck.

Make a small loop, (crochet chain or buttonhole bar), on each side of the shoulder and sew a button at the opposite side to fasten. Make a cord to thread through the holes at the waist and finish off by crocheting a neat edge around each sleeve in a contrasting green.

Panties

These are green too! Cast on 5sts and work 2 rows of ss.

Continue to work in ss, but increase one st at each end of rows 3, 7, 9, 11, 13, 14, 15, 16 and 17. Then work straight until a total of 22 rows have been completed.

Row 23 to 25: single rib.

Cast off and make another piece in the same way. Sew up the narrow edges between the two legs and at each side.

Headscarf

This is simply a large triangular piece of garter stitch with a cord fixed to each corner.

Cast on 2sts and knit them.

Now inc at each end of *every row* until there are 24sts.

Now inc at each end every alt row until there are 40 sts.

Inc at each end of every row until there are 60sts.

Cast off. Neaten the edges by working a row of crochet along the sides and then attach cords to each corner.

Knitting know-how

Every knitter, no matter how expert, needs to be
reminded of the endless possibilities the craft
can offer. Just reading about something you may already
know jogs the memory and generates ideas.
This chapter will help you with such details as
picking up stitches from edges, instead of seaming them,
and suggest ways of embroidering features
and tiny details with duplicate stitch.

Abbreviations

alt	alternate
beg	begin(ning)
cm	centimetre(s)
ch	crochet chain(s)
dec	decrease
dc	double crochet (US single crochet)
DK	double knitting yarn
g st	garter stitch
gm	gramme(s)
in	inch(es)
inc	increase
k	knit
k2tog	knit two stitches together to decrease
LH	left hand
k-wise	in a knitwise direction
m	metre(s)
mm	millimetres
No	number(s)
oz	ounce(s)
patt	pattern
p	purl
p2tog	purl two stitches together to decrease
p-wise	in a purlwise direction
psso	pass the slip stitch over
rev ss	reversed stocking stitch
rem	remain(ing)
rep	repeat
RH	right hand
RS	right side of fabric
sl 1	slip one stitch without knitting it
st	stitch(es)
ss	stocking stitch (US stockinette stitch)
tog	together
WS	wrong side of fabric
y bk	yarn to the back
yd	yard(s)
y fwd	yarn forward
yrn	yarn round needle

Symbols used

A single asterisk, *, in the row indicates that the stitches following this sign are to be repeated as directed.

Instructions given in round brackets, ( ), are to be repeated as many times as the number which follows them.

Stitches

The examples used in this book are all very simple techniques, even for beginners or children.

Loose cast on

This is also known as Shetland cast on and is a particularly useful method where one needs to pick up stitches from a cast on edge to work in the opposite direction, or to make a border, as it leaves loops. As the diagram shows, see Fig 1, to make each new stitch, the needle is entered into the one just made. Compare this with the conventional cast on below.

fig 1 **loose cast on**

Firm cast on (no diagram given)

For a firm and neat edge, make each new stitch by entering the needle *between* the first two stitches, (i.e nearest the point), on the LH needle.

Gathering the last stitches on to a wool needle

Instead of casting off, one sometimes needs to draw up the last stitches on to a thread, prior to gathering them. This is done by cutting off the yarn to leave a longish end and threading this into a wool-needle. Slide the stitches off, a few at a time, on to the needle and down the yarn, see Fig 2. To hold the gathered stitches firmly, take the needle through them a second time and pull gently.

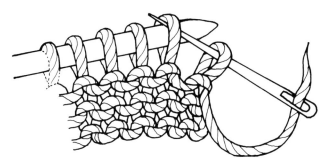

fig 2 **gathering last sts on to wool needle**

Swiss darning, or duplicate stitch

Many knitters find it more convenient to embroider small areas of pattern on to a piece of knitting, rather than knit it in with short lengths of yarn. Duplicate stitch is an apt name as, when done with care, the effect is indistinguishable from stocking stitch. It is also useful for adding extra touches, which were not originally allowed for at a later date and also for rectifying mistakes.

Begin by running the new thread into the wrong side of the piece, bringing the blunt-ended sewing needle and thread out in the centre of one V-shape. Note the RH bottom corner of the diagram, see Fig 3. Take the needle up to the stitch immediately above this one and round the back, (in and out again), of it as shown. Now the needle goes back into the first one, (i.e the one it started from), and at the same time moves one stitch to the left, working from right to left and coming out in the centre of the next V. This follows the track of the real stitch which it is covering. Each new stitch lays over the one underneath, so take care not to pull the thread too tightly and, if necessary, adjust it with the point of the needle as you go along.

fig 3 **Swiss darning or duplicate st**

Basic stitches

Garter stitch

On size 4mm needles with DK yarn, 5sts + 10 rows = 2.5cm (1in).
Every row is knitted. This stitch needs more rows per cm/in than most other stitches and it also expands sideways, so needs fewer stitches. It is, however, a good dense stitch which lies flat and does not curl.

Stocking stitch

On size 4mm needles with DK yarn, 5sts + 8 rows = 2.5cm (1in). (American, stockinette stitch.)
Alternate rows knitted and purled. Smooth surface on one side, rough on the other. Be prepared to make use of *both* sides. Changes of colour always link on the purl side, showing a mixture of colours, so beware of this. Grows quickly but curls inwards on to the purl side – this can be a nuisance but the remedy is to work an edge of 4 or 5 moss sts on larger pieces. To make sewing up easier, begin every row with one knit stitch.

Single rib

On size 4mm needles with DK yarn, 13sts + 15 rows = 5cm (2in).
Alternate stitches knit and purl on an even number of stitches, beginning every row with a knit stitch.

This is a guide, not a rule. Makes an elastic fabric with pronounced vertical ridges. Firm, does not curl, but *does* contract inwards considerably, so extra stitches are needed to compensate. Good for leaves and tiny plants.

Double rib

On size 4mm needles with DK yarn, 16sts + 15 rows = 5cm (2in).
K2, p2 worked alternately in pairs, usually over multiples of 4 stitches, but see note below.
Produces thick, vertical ridges also contracts, (see single rib). Makes good soil ridges and decorative brickwork.

Moss stitch

On size 4mm needles with DK yarn, 5sts + 9 rows = 2.5cm (1in).
On an odd number of stitches, every row begins k1, p1.

Produces a tiny pebble effect, behaves well without curling but tends to spread sideways.

Double moss stitch

On size 4mm needles with DK yarn, 11sts + 18 rows = 5cm (2in).

This version is worked over multiple of 4 stitches and 4 rows, first 2 beginning k2, p2, and second 2 beginning p2, k2. Makes a strong bubble pattern and texture, useful for walls, paving, etc, but spreads sideways. Beware of over-estimating number of stitches.

Note: once the structure of these stitch patterns is understood, one is no longer bound by a certain number of stitches, e.g moss st *can* be worked on an even number and single rib on an odd number. Just keep the stitches in the correct order.

Knitted fur loop stitch

Only two movements are illustrated although six stages are required to complete each stitch.

This pattern tends to be denser than its crochet counterpart, as the yarn is wrapped several times round the fingers to make multiple loops each time. Multiple strands of yarn can be used to make even more loops but thicker needles should be used to cope with this extra bulk. The loops are worked on alternate rows, hanging down on the side farthest away from you; the in-between rows are knitted. Cast on an even number of stitches and knit the first row.

A. Enter the needle into the first stitch in the usual way. Extend two fingers of the LH while keeping hold of the needle with the other.

B. Wrap the yarn round the two fingers as shown in the diagram, see Fig 1b, over the top and under, two or three times.

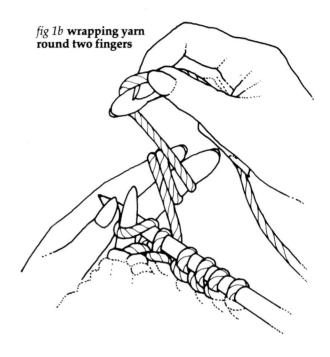

fig 1b **wrapping yarn round two fingers**

C. As it comes up for the last time, take it over the point of the LH needle and complete the stitch.

D. Now enter the RH needle into the loops on the fingers, yarn over, and make another complete stitch, allowing the loops to drop down on to the far side. Hold them down with the fingers, see Fig 1d.

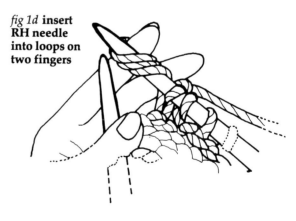

fig 1d **insert RH needle into loops on two fingers**

E. A decrease must now be made, as you have two stitches in place of one, so pass the first stitch over the top of the second, as in casting off, using the point of the LH needle.

F. Knit the next stitch. Continue in this way to the end of the row, making a knit stitch in between each loop stitch. Knit the next row straight.

The loops can be left as loops or they can be cut open for a furry effect.

Useful embroidery stitches

Running stitch is used extensively on our small projects, for gathering up the ends of knitted pieces like hands, feet, heads, etc. Work them as near to the edge as possible, except for necks and waists, making them evenly-spaced and regular. Use a blunt-ended wool needle to avoid splitting the yarn. The same yarn which was used for the gathering/running stitch can also be used to continue the sewing-up process, see Fig 2.

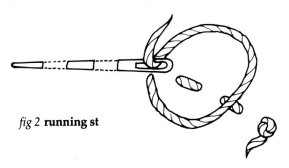

fig 2 **running st**

Satin stitch is very useful for small details such as eyes and mouths. On very small pieces, DK yarn is usually too thick and I prefer to use stranded cotton, or finer 2 or 3 ply yarns. A pointed needle can be used for this purpose as accuracy is vitally important. This stitch can also be used to make tiny pointed ears and beaks, by piling up the stitches one on top of the other and pulling each one firmly until the required height is reached, see Fig 3.

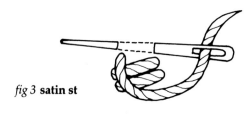

fig 3 **satin st**

Picking up stitches

It is not always necessary to cast on new stitches for each new unit; 'knitting on', or 'crocheting on' is much easier, as it avoids both the cast on and the sewing up processes. It also ensures that exactly the correct number of stitches is available for the new piece to be made. Picking up stitches is easily done in both knitting and crochet from any edge, even a woven fabric at the top, bottom or sides, making a very neat and attractive transition from one unit to another.

Here are some hints for you to follow. If you haven't done it before, give it a try; you will soon find that it speeds things up wonderfully.

1. Always use a smooth yarn for picking up new stitches as fuzzy or bumpy ones make extra problems.
2. Use a yarn of similar thickness as the one on the 'host' piece, as thicker ones cause distortion.
3. Needles and hooks should also be of about the same size as those used on the 'host' piece, though on some occasions you may find that a finer tool does the picking up row more easily. However, for subsequent rows one should change back to the normal size to avoid distortion.
4. Keep the supply yarn in the left hand instead of in the right as in normal knitting, and use it as you would if you were crocheting. Don't let this put you off though; do whatever is most comfortable.
5. Always pick up stitches with the right side of the work facing you, as the process makes a ridge which is best left on the wrong side.
6. To join in the new yarn, you can work any of these methods:–
   a. Loop it over the needle, or hook, and leave a longish end to be darned in later.
   b. As above, but carry the end along with you on the second row and weave it in behind, or, if a purl row, on the front.
   c. If there is an 'end' already at the point where you will begin picking up new stitches, tie the new yarn to this and keep going. This means that you will have to knit through the knot, leaving it at the back of the row until you can weave it in.
   d. There may be a loop available which you can use as your first stitch, perhaps one left at the end of a cast off row. This can be used for travelling in the same direction as before or for going down the side edge. For this reason it is always a good idea to leave long ends before cutting off the supply yarn.

Opposite: Here you can clearly see details of the different stitch patterns which have been used for the cottages and gardens.

Picking up stitches in knitting

1. From a knitted cast on edge, this is where the loose, (Shetland), cast on comes in useful as here are loops ready and waiting for you to put your needle into. If you have to work into a firmer cast on edge, separate out one strand for each stitch and knit into this. The tension should be exactly the same.

2. From a knitted cast off edge, pick up the stitches as shown in the diagram, see Fig 1, sliding the needle under both strands of the stitch, loop the yarn over the point and pull this loop through to the right side. Leave it on the needle. You should have exactly the same number of stitches as the 'host' piece.

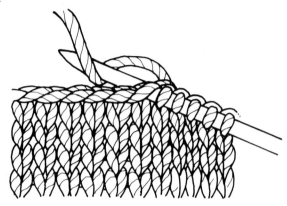

fig 1 **picking up sts in knitting from a knitted cast-off edge**

3. From a side edge (the selvedge), put the needle into the knitted fabric between every two rows, whether this is on stocking stitch or garter stitch. This should give you a correct tension equal to the host piece.

4. To knit into the top or bottom edges of crochet, see Fig 2, pick up the chain space with the needle, using both strands on the top edge but noting that only one strand will be available on the bottom edge. The main point to remember here is that crochet stitches are fatter than knitted ones, so you will need *more* knit stitches than the chain spaces on

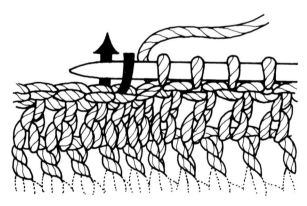

fig 2 **knitting into the top or bottom edge of crochet**

the host piece. If you are using the same yarn thickness and hook size, estimate that you will need about one-third more knit stitches, so make 2sts into every 3rd chain space. This is an increase of one in every 3sts. If you find this difficult to do, make your increases on the first knit row instead, increasing once into every 3rd stitch.

5. To knit into a crochet side edge may be a little more tricky, as the sides of crochet stitches are less dense and more straggly than knitted edges. However, it can be done, though the rules are less defined. Estimate the number of stitches you will need, (check your knitted tension for this then measure the crochet edge), and mark with pins along the edge at 2.5cm (1in) intervals. You should then be able to space your pick-up stitches between these pins fairly accurately. Put the hook into anything available, trying to keep your stitches as level and as even as possible.

Picking up stitches in crochet

1. When working into a knitted cast on or cast off edge, see Fig 3, the loops are not usually quite large enough for the hook to slide under easily, except with the loose cast on method. So the hook must be entered below the ridge as shown in the diagram. Remember though that you will not need as many crochet stitches as the knitted ones, because crochet stitches are fatter. Estimate that you will need only about two-thirds of the number on the host piece, and space them out accordingly. This means that you can miss out every third space but only if you are using the same thickness of yarn and corresponding hook size as the original.

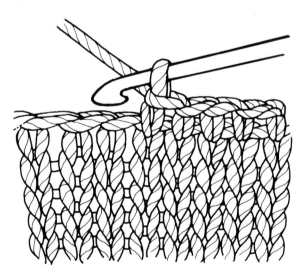

fig 3 **picking up sts in crochet from a knitted edge**

2. To crochet into a knitted selvedge, enter the hook into the same part of each stitch along the edge to keep the depth of the new stitches regular, and use pins as markers to make sure that your new stitches

are spaced evenly. Check as you proceed that your tension is correct and adjust this accordingly.

3. To crochet into the base chain and work in the opposite direction, the chain of crochet has loops ready for the hook to use, so working in the opposite direction is no problem. Incidentally, the same can be said about knitting, however, only one loop will be available, instead of two, so take care not to pull this out of shape.

4. To crochet into the side edge of crochet is about as tricky as knitting into it! The hints are the same as in No 5 in the previous section.

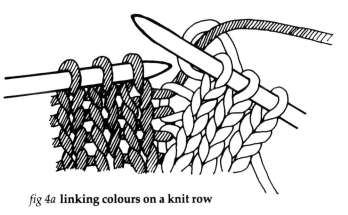

fig 4a **linking colours on a knit row**

Two-colour knitting

When using more than one colour in a row, it is not always necessary to strand or weave the extra yarns behind if they are to be used only in that one position, but unless great care is taken to link two adjoining colours together as they pass, a hole is likely to occur.

To avoid this happening, link the two colours on a knit row as shown in the diagram, see Fig 4a and on a purl row Fig 4b, by taking the new colour underneath the old one before making the stitch. Do this on every row. 'Tails' of new colours can be woven in along the back for a few stitches, or darned in at a later date.

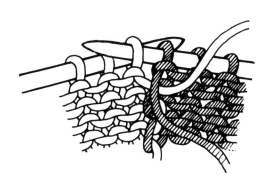

fig 4b **linking colours on a purl row**

Sewing up

In projects of this nature, attaching small pieces to each other is not quite the same as dealing with garment seams. Here, we can be a little less fraught about it all, though still exact enough to use pins wherever possible. Always use the same thickness of yarn, too, for sewing up and darn ends in neatly.

The two seams described here are adequate for the projects in this book, although the overcast seam finds little favour with some knitting purists. The flat seam is used by emroiderers in constructional techniques and is of great use when things have to be joined together from the right side.

1. Overcast seam, see Fig 5, is made on the wrong side of the fabric with the two pieces placed RS together. It can also be made with the pieces flat out and edge-to-edge if necessary. Pin pieces first.

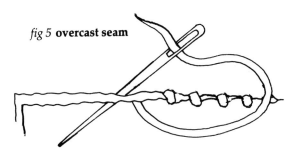

fig 5 **overcast seam**

2. Flat seam, see Fig 6, is most useful when sewing up must be done from the RS, as when a cushion pad is being stitched into place in a cover. It is also very neat and should be almost invisible. Place the fabric flat down, or in its final position, edge-to-edge and with the RS uppermost. After fixing the thread, take the needle under each side of the join alternately, (you will need to use both hands for

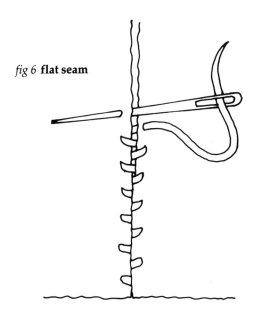

fig 6 **flat seam**

this), first towards the left and then towards the right. Only half of each stitch will be seen as the other half will be underneath the opposite side. Keep the tension even and the stitches close together.

3. In sewing up tiny pieces accuracy is essential, as with so few rows and stitches, the odd one missed out may make all the difference. Check the effect from stitch to stitch and be prepared to go back and re-do the seam.

4. In joining stripes you must take care to match these carefully when sewing up as, unfortunately, in-accuracies show more on small things than they do on big ones. Where they occur, place pins on the WS so that you are warned ahead of their approach.

5. Darning-in is not discussed within the instructions for each of the projects, as it will obviously be understood that this should be done neatly and efficiently to avoid little fingers, (and big ones too!), getting accidently caught up in the ends.

Long 'tails' from the cast on and off edges can be used for sewing up, so don't chop these off short until you are sure they are no longer needed. New yarns introduced along the row, whether the same or another colour, can either be knotted and the knot left on the wrong side, or simply looped over to make the new stitch. In both cases, the ends can be darned or woven in on the back.

Index